DIGITAL POVERTY:
Latin American and Caribbean Perspectives

Practical
ACTION
PUBLISHING

International Development Research Centre
Ottawa • Cairo • Dakar • Montevideo • Nairobi • New Delhi • Singapore

Practical Action Publishing Ltd
25 Albert Street, Rugby, CV21 2SD, Warwickshire, UK
www.practicalactionpublishing.com

and the International Development Research Centre
P.O. Box 8500, Ottawa, ON, Canada K1G 3HP
www.idrc.ca/info@idrc.ca

ISBN 978-1-85339-663-2
ISBN ebook 9781780441115
Book DOI: https://doi.org/10.3362/9781780441115

First published in 2007

A catalogue record for this book is available from the British Library.

The contributors have asserted their rights under the Copyright Designs and Patents Act 1988 to be identified as authors of their respective contributions.

Since 1974, Practical Action Publishing has published and disseminated books and information in sup-port of international development work throughout the world. Practical Action Publishing (formerly ITDG Publishing) is a trading name of Intermediate Technology Publications Ltd (Company Reg. No. 1159018), the wholly owned publishing company of Intermediate Technology Development Group Ltd (working name Practical Action). Practical Action Publishing trades only in support of its parent chari-ty objectives and any profits are covenanted back to Practical Action (Charity Reg. No. 247257, Group VAT Registration No. 880 9924 76).

Cover photograph with kind permission from IDRC

Cover by Mercer Design
Designed and typeset by Forma Estudio, Montevideo, Uruguay
Reasonable efforts have been made to publish reliable data and information, but the author and publisher cannot assume responsibility for the validity of all materials or for the consequences of their use.

The manufacturer's authorised representative in the EU for product safety is Lightning Source France, 1 Av. Johannes Gutenberg, 78310 Maurepas, France. compliance@lightningsource.fr

Table of Contents

The Regional Dialogue on the Information Society (REDIS-DIRSI)

REDIS-DIRSI is a regional network of leading researchers and institutions concerned with the creation and dissemination of knowledge that supports effective participation in the Information Society by the poor. Through its collaborative structure, REDIS-DIRSI aims to become the focal point for research and learning about pro-poor ICT policies and regulation in the region, cultivating partnerships with donors, multilateral agencies, universities, regulators, and civil society organizations.

REDIS-DIRSI
Instituto de Estudios Peruanos, Horacio Urteaga 694, Lima 11 PERU
Web: www.dirsi.net

Foreword

Ben Petrazzini

IDRC is an organization that is in constant search for excellence and innovation: excellence and innovation in applied research aimed at improving the lives of those that are less resourced and in most need.

It is under this broad framework and with those goals in mind that in November 2004, IDRC through one of its initiatives (the Institute for Connectivity in the Americas – ICA – www.icamericas.net) convened in Montevideo a group of top social scientists from Latin America and the Caribbean to revisit and critically assess the challenges and opportunities posed by the rise of the information economy and society in the region.

The event was the first step in Latin America and the Caribbean (LAC) to respond to the recommendations of an IDRC Forum that brought information and communication technologies (ICT) leaders from around the world to Harvard University in September of 2003. The Harvard Forum identified ICT policy and regulation as one of the key bottlenecks in addressing the inequalities associated with the digital divide.

The underlying principle of the initiative that ensued was that policy and regulatory design in this sector requires policy makers to pay attention to the needs of marginalized and low income communities (pro-poor) without losing sight of the fact that competition and market forces are in most cases a powerful tool to bring down prices and increase access to services (pro-market).

With the "pro-poor, pro-market" concept as background, and with the agreed-upon notion that ICT policy and regulatory reform have entered in recent times a period of stagnation, the authors of this book set for themselves the challenge of thinking "out of the box" and exploring new strategies to help address the challenges posed by the digital poverty that affects the LAC region.

In the process, as collaboration and shared work began to unfold, a regional network of policy professionals began to take shape. By June 2005 (thanks to the support of Pan Americas, another IDRC initiative in the area of ICT in LAC) the Regional Dialogue on the Information Society (REDIS-DIRSI) became a reality. By October 2005 after months of solid and sound work, we are witnessing the publication of the first book of the network. The reader will find in this volume the seeds of creative thinking that will surely stimulate the rise of valuable policy debates and will contribute in a significant way to the exploration of innovative ICT solutions for the region.

IDRC hopes that initiatives like this one will become, with time, a driving force in the generation of innovative and locally sound policies and strategies to bridge the digital divide among and within countries.

Ben Petrazzini
SENIOR PROGRAM SPECIALIST
INSTITUTE FOR CONNECTIVITY IN THE AMERICAS
INTERNATIONAL DEVELOPMENT RESEARCH CENTRE

Introduction

by Judith Mariscal and Hernan Galperin

Over the past two decades, market reforms in the Information and Communication Technologies (ICT) sector have served as a powerful engine for infrastructure investments and service expansion in developing nations. More people have gained access to ICT services since market reforms started in the early 1990s than in the many decades that preceded these reforms. The economic and social benefits have been manifold. As the telephone, the Internet, and even older ICT such as broadcasting became more accessible and generally more affordable, more people began using them to access new markets and be more productive, to seek better healthcare, to take advantage of lifelong educational opportunities, to strengthen family and community bonds, and to demand better services and more accountability from their governments.

Nonetheless there continue to be large numbers of people and communities without adequate access to ICT in the developing world. This book examines the different dimensions of this problem from the vantage point of the experience in Latin America and the Caribbean. As the chapters that follow reveal, further market reforms are clearly needed in many cases. However, these chapters also reveal the limitations of market reforms to ensure that the benefits of the Information Society penetrate across the multiple social and economic divides that characterize the region. In the rush to attract private investments, privatize inefficient operators and establish new industry regulators, the adequate supply of ICT services to the more vulnerable sectors of the population and the more isolated communities was, for much of the 1990s, relegated to the policy backburner.

This book represents the first publication of the Regional Dialogue on the Information Society (DIRSI), a regional network of leading researchers concerned with the creation and dissemination of knowledge that supports effective participation in the Information Society by the poor and marginalized communities of Latin America and the Caribbean. The chapters that follow reflect a diverse set of studies undertaken by DIRSI members under the common theme of pro-poor, pro-market ICT policies. This theme seeks to support next-generation policy reforms that build on the achievements of market liberalization efforts but at the same time address the realities of what we call *digital poverty* – a concept that seeks to grasp the multiple dimensions of inadequate levels of access to ICT services by people and organizations, as well as the barriers to their productive use.

To be sure, some Latin American and Caribbean countries have been pioneers in the implementation of universal access programs, and have attained impressive results in the provision of ICT access to underserved segments of the population. However, we believe the time is right to make a leap forward towards an effective ICT adoption in Latin America and the Caribbean as well as other developing regions of the world. Towards this end we must seize the opportunity offered by the lessons learned from the first and second generation of reforms, by the technological innovations that are taking place in the sector, and by the increased visibility of ICT access inequalities.

We now know that access is a necessary step towards ICT adoption but it is not sufficient in itself. ICTs are technological tools that require training; human capacity is a prerequisite for adoption. Internet access is useful only if content is meaningful; if local actors participate in its implementation making sure it addresses local needs. The aim of this book is to initiate the leap towards a new perspective on ICT access, and to develop an analytical framework that examines the critical variables involved in effective ICT adoption in developing regions of the world.

The chapters tackle both theoretical and practical questions related to ICT governance and policies in the region. The first two chapters by Barja and Gigler (chapter 1) and Barrantes (chapter 2) develop a conceptual foundation for the measurement of digital or information poverty in the Latin American and Caribbean context. Both seek to define the notions of poverty in general as well as the concept of digital poverty in particular. Attention is paid not only to the demand for connectivity itself but also to the demand for its attributes, namely, information and communication, with the goal of conceptualizing the different types of uses related to connectivity.

Barja and Gigler build their analysis on the poverty line locality criteria for the identification of information and communication poverty, suggesting tools to study its magnitude, depth and characteristics. They also suggest approaches to measure the economic cost individual localities face to reach this line, and thereby to assess the access gap between localities. Barrantes on the other hand identifies three major causes for digital poverty: lack of supply, lack of demand and lack of need or capacity to use ICT. She points towards the need to design public policies specifically targeting each of these causes. Her approach for measuring digital poverty is based on models used for estimating unfulfilled basic needs rather than on those used to identify poverty thresholds. Both papers suggest that the concept of digital poverty has a number of implications for public policy design, particularly in the definition of incentives and restrictions most conducive to meaningful participation by those presently excluded from ICT.

The second set of chapters move into the realm of the practical governance questions faced by regulators in the region. In chapter 3, Mariscal, Bonina and Luna present evidence about the powerful combination of mobile telephony and prepaid business models for increasing teledensity among the poor. Yet she also warns that regulators may be ill-equipped to address the implications of increased industry consolidation in mobile and fixed telephony into two large regional players (Telefónica and Telmex). Similarly, Dussán and Roldán Perea (chapter 4) reveal that the institutional design of national regulators generally leads to inadequate participation by civil society and consumer interest groups in the decision-making process, thus making agencies more vulnerable to be captured by industry and less responsive to the concerns of politically disenfranchised groups. In both cases, recommendations are made to strengthen regulatory capacity to address these outstanding challenges.

The third group of chapters provide evidence about existing – and replicable – models to provide ICT services to rural communities and other underserved areas. Galperin and Girard describe new models and possibilities for the local provision of network services. Their research suggests that microtelcos – small-scale telecom operators that combine local entrepreneurship, municipal efforts, and community action – can and do play an important role in addressing the ICT needs of the poor. They describe the experience of a variety of microtelcos – led by local entrepreneurs, cooperatives, and municipal governments – that are effectively servicing many underserved areas in different countries in the region. Their paper also explores the enabling role of new technologies, such as wireless local area networks (WLANs), for microtelcos to extend ICT services into areas unattractive to conventional operators. Finally, they identify the need for an enabling regulatory environment and analyze existing regulatory constraints for microtelcos, suggesting alternatives to remove these obstacles within a framework of technologically-neutral market rules.

The Percolator Model outlined by Mallalieu and Rocke follows a similar conceptual trajectory by providing a framework within which development-oriented ICT solutions may be contemplated in a systematic and manageable way. The model takes into account a) key developmental objectives and the political-cultural context (base domain), b) the technical requirements derived from the attributes of ICT within a social context (user domain) and c) the technical features of available ICT (technology domain). It offers a compelling solution tree based on contextual and technical parameters that can guide the customized selection of appropriate ICT for underserved communities. The study also provides a detailed comparison of existing and future ICT solutions that percolate up from the different domains of the model.

The concluding chapter by Mahan reviews and unites the different themes raised in the previous chapters from a pro-poor perspective. She addresses ICT demand and supply side issues, regulatory reforms and the private sector, consumer advocacy, new ownership models for network service provision and emerging network technology solutions. The chapter also provides the context for assessing various digital or information poverty indicators in the Latin American and Caribbean region, as well as for exploring the existing regulatory framework and its limitations. Mahan also stresses the importance of research efforts (such as those of DIRSI) in advancing knowledge about ICT demand and supply, universal service models, and regulatory tools that improve the design of public policies that promote access, participation and digital empowerment by the poor. This book is an attempt in this direction, which we hope will contribute to a multi-stakeholder dialogue about promoting ICT policies for poverty reduction in the region.

There are many people who played an important role in bringing together this group of scholars that formed the basis for the launch of the DIRSI network (now extended to several new members), and without whom this book would not have been possible. We would first like to acknowledge Ben Petrazzini and his team at the Institute for Connectivity in the Americas (ICA-IDRC), as well as Alicia Richero and her team at Pan Americas-IDRC for their financial and intellectual support in the creation of DIRSI and the completion of the research projects that are compiled in this book. We would also like to thank friends and other members of the DIRSI network who participated in the discussion and review of earlier manuscripts, in particular Hopeton Dunn, Leonardo Mena, Michele Rioux, Marlon Tabora, Martin Hilbert and Marcio Wohlers. Finally, we acknowledge the assistance of Francisco Gutierrez, Julio Luna, Olga Cavalli and Carla Bonina in coordinating the editorial and production process.

CHAPTER 1

The Concept of Information Poverty and How to Measure it in the Latin American Context

Gover Barja
UNIVERSIDAD CATÓLICA BOLIVIANA

Björn-Sören Gigler
LONDON SCHOOL OF ECONOMICS

Abstract

The construction of the information society must be complemented with pro-poor vision and policies. For this reason, this paper defines the concept of information and communication poverty, introduces the criteria of poverty line location for its identification, and suggests computation for the economic cost of reaching such a line for its aggregate measurement. In this process, the structural and technological restrictions faced by a society are acknowledged, and the way they affect and are affected by the concept of information and communication poverty is discussed. This research study examines these issues conceptually, in order to contribute to the study regarding magnitude, depth and characteristics of information and communication poverty, as well as to identify some of its implications for drafting public policies.

1. Introduction

An important consequence of globalization is that growth of small open economies increasingly depend on their internal and external competitiveness. As a consequence public policy in Latin America tends to focus primarily on improving the competitiveness of its economies and of the region. However, this economic growth paradigm based on pro-competitiveness policies does not guarantee, by itself, a solution to the multiple challenges of reducing poverty. For this reason, pro-growth policies must be complemented by pro-poor policies.

This chapter is based on the hypothesis that an information society based on pro-growth policies must be complemented by pro-poor policies. This work focuses only on the aspect related to the need to develop pro-poor policies that accompany, complement and strengthen the process of constructing an information society.

In order to develop these pro-poor policies, it is necessary to carefully define the meaning of information and communication poverty, its relation to the construction of the information society, its connection to poverty-reducing policies and its contribution to development. This issue is developed in the second section of this chapter. The third section develops criteria to define poverty in terms of a person's lack of information and communication capabilities, and identifies criteria to measure and evaluate aggregate information poverty. These criteria are the main contribution of this chapter. In a manner similar to literature on poverty, the reasons for its measurement are to inform society on its magnitude and depth, its causes and consequences, as well as to contribute to the drafting of pro-poor public policies. This section also acknowledges a society's technological and structural constraints regarding the way they affect and are affected by information and communication poverty. The fourth section presents conclusions and some implications.

2. What is Poverty and what is Information and Communication Poverty

2.1. DEVELOPMENT, POVERTY AND INEQUALITY

In its broad definition, development is the process of expansion of human freedoms. Sen's point of view (2000) establishes that the expansion of freedoms is development's means and ultimate goal. Among the freedoms highlighted by Sen as development means are: political freedom[1], economic facilities[2], social opportunities[3],

---

[1] People's opportunities to determine who should govern and under which principles, freedom to evaluate and criticize authorities, freedom of expression, right to dialogue, to oppose, to criticize, to vote, to choose among political parties, to be involved in Legislative and Executive elections.

[2] An individual's opportunities to use economic resources with the purpose of consumption, production or exchange. The economic ownership of a person depends on the possession of resources, use availability, exchange conditions and its distribution.

[3] It refers to the way a society organizes itself to provide education, health and social services, which contribute to an effective participation on political and economic activities.

transparency guarantees[4], protective security[5] and the significant and complementary relationships among them. These freedoms strengthen an individual's capability; poverty is, from this point of view, the lack of basic capabilities. Thus, an adequate multidimensional assessment of the improvement observed on the standard of living of the poor must analyze their achievements and obtained capabilities.

In practice, due to information restrictions and the long-term impact on poverty, assessments conducted on poverty reduction have been focused on more limited variables, such as income or expenditure patterns of the poor. Traditional methodologies are based on defining a set of criteria to identify the poor and assessing aggregate poverty.

For example, Ravallion (2000) defines the absolute criterion of living on one dollar and two dollars per day, as a line to identify the poor. Then, he measures aggregate poverty by the ratio of individuals below that line, as well as the sum of distances to that line as the poverty gap. Dollar and Kraay (2000) apply the income of the poorest fifth as a relative criterion to identify the poor. They then measure aggregate poverty according to per-capita income in this group. The World Bank Institute's experience (Online, 2005) indicates that the consumption expenditure criterion[6] may be more appropriate for the identification of the poor than the income criterion. It suggests establishing a poverty line based on a basic food expenditure method that takes into account the minimum calorie intake needed by a person per day, or the basic needs basket method, which includes expenditures on food and non-food basic items; aggregate poverty is then measured according to the FGT Index[7] or the SST Index[8].

Although monetary income/consumption has the benefit of being quantifiable, it can only be considered an approximation of an individual's welfare, since it does not make any reference to the quality of life, from Sen's point of view. Other approaches are based on resource availability, represented by pragmatic variables such as income per capita and individual available income, or by primary goods, a more theoretical but broader variable[9]. Robeyns (2004) is rather conciliatory when

---

[4] It refers to the fact that social interaction is based on the basic assumption of confidence. Such expected confidence guarantees an open and clear attitude among involved parties, contributing to prevent corruption, financial irresponsibility and obscure agreements.

[5] It refers to a vulnerable situation people may be experiencing, which requires safety nets, unemployment benefits, income for the needy, and emergency funds.

[6] Usually making adjustments for durable goods, housing services, size and composition of home.

[7] Foster, Greer and Thorbecke (1984) introduced a set of parametric poverty measurements which generates three poverty indicators: ratio of poor, poverty gap and poverty severity.

[8] Sen, Shorrocks and Thon (World Bank Institute, 2005) introduced an index computed according to the indicators of ratio of poor, digital divide and Gini's coefficient.

[9] Also called Rawlsian goods: those every rational person would wish – income, wealth, opportunities and social base of self-respect.

suggesting that these different approaches (monetary, resource and capability) should be viewed as complementary in terms of poverty measurement, poverty analysis (micro or macro) and relevance, depending on the type of poverty analysis.

The work *An Asset-Based Approach to the Analysis of Poverty*, by Attanasio and Székely (1999), derived from the approaches mentioned above, states that the structural causes of poverty depend mainly on:

- Ownership of income-earning assets, which can be physical assets (housing and basic services), human assets (health, education) or social assets (social networks and rules).

- Rate of asset-use, since the higher the use, the higher the income (employment opportunity, gender, credit access).

Based on this approach, the authors conclude that social policy should aim at generating income by increasing household assets, creating opportunities for productive asset use, and increasing their market prices.

In this context of varying conceptual approaches to poverty, a specific question arises regarding the causes and characteristics of poverty in Latin America[10]. Székely (2001) points out that poverty in Latin America is not mainly due to a lack of resources to fulfill basic needs, but to income distribution inequality. The question inferred from this statement is: What is the reason for an inadequate income distribution in Latin America? According to Attanasio and Székely (2001), approximately one third of the inequality is based on personal variables such as education level, age, gender, region, occupation, economic activity, etc. The other two-thirds are based on economic structural aspects, which are repeated at all economic levels: city, municipality, state and region.

These observations on inequality are of particular interest when considering that the concept of development is based on the traditional economic growth paradigm. Dollar and Kraay (2000) point out that economic growth also benefits the poor in a one-to-one relationship; thus, specific policies for poverty reduction are not justified. In contrast, Bourguignon (2001) shows that growth elasticity of poverty is a decreasing function of the development level obtained by an economy, as well as a decreasing function of the inequality level of relative income.

In addition, Lora, Pagés, Panizza and Stein (2004) conclude that the structural reforms may not have improved poverty and inequality conditions, since they did not attack their causes, namely, the lack of access by the poor to credit and to assets which increase their productivity. They also point out that poverty and inequality reduction policies should focus on releasing the poor's growth potential, facilitating

---

[10] There is a vast literature on poverty, more than exposed here, which reflects a permanent state of debate.

their acquisition of productive assets by ensuring such assets during times of crisis and increasing their access. Székely (2001) also concludes that economic growth, by itself, does not solve the poverty problem. For this reason, pro-growth policies must be complemented and strengthened by pro-poor policies. These policies should address the structural causes of poverty[11], and should be large-scale in order to have a significant impact on the society (social policy)[12], contributing in this way to long-term growth[13]. A key question in the information society context is: What role does access to information and communication through ICT play within the structural causes of poverty? As many authors have emphasized (Kenny, 2003; Gigler, 2001 and 2005; McNamara, 2000 and 2003), the present discussion about the 'digital divide' focuses on the analysis of the access level of different groups (i.e. the connectivity level of women or minority groups in a society) and does not reflect the reasons that cause the existing gap. For this reason, this paper focuses on the definition of information and communication poverty, to attain a better comprehension of the key factors that determine if a society is prepared to take advantage of ICT for economic development and poverty reduction.

2.2. CONCEPT OF INFORMATION AND COMMUNICATION POVERTY

There is no need to develop an independent theory for the information society; in turn, the existing theory should be applied to clarify a particular aspect of poverty and development. From this discussion we can foresee that the construction of the information society would naturally be based on the pro-growth approach, as reflected by the pro-competitiveness indicators published by the World Economic Forum (2004). This chapter argues, however, that the creation of the information society should be complemented by a pro-poor approach to avoid the increase in inequalities and social exclusion, specifically in Latin America, a region with high levels of social and economic inequalities and low levels of economic and human development.

It may also be suggested that, in the broadest sense, the expansion of human freedoms must also be the means and ultimate goal in the construction of the information society, as a way of contributing to development. These freedoms will strengthen the individuals' capability to participate in the information society and therefore the communication and information poverty is a lack of the basic capabilities needed to participate in the information society.

---

[11] These pro-poor policies should not be relief or protection programs for the poor during times of crisis, or safety nets, as these are circumstantial and do not attack the causes of poverty. Usually the programs focused on income work over consequences without changing causes.

[12] Programs with a limited impact could not be used either, even if they attacked structural causes of poverty, since they have a limited impact by focusing on reduced groups of society.

[13] Pro-poor policies must be consistent with pro-growth policies, and not oppose them.

As Gigler (2005) has pointed out, information is not only a source of knowledge, but also a special source of advancement of economic, social, political, and cultural freedoms. It can be said that access to and use of information and communications are essential conditions for development, as they affect every dimension of life. Likewise, information and communication poverty may only be one dimension of poverty, but affects all other dimensions. For that reason its effective reduction is interdependent on the other dimensions.

We must add to the discussion the origin of the information society, which results from the continual technological revolution observed in the field of the information and communication technologies. However, as Easterly (2003) highlights, nothing happens when technology is available but the incentives to use it are not present. In particular, Easterly indicates the need of intervention to compensate the disincentives to technological innovation[14].

3. Measurement of Information and Communication Poverty

3.1. POVERTY LINE

The need for advancement in freedoms ΔL^i must be the result of the difference between the desired demand of freedoms L^i_1 and the current freedoms achieved L^i_0 for each kind i: $\Delta L^i = L^i_1 - L^i_0$. The requirement of expansion of each kind of freedom is not the same, as some of them may be more desired than others according to the circumstances.

This approach highlights L^i_0, as it is what a society has achieved and, therefore, the minimum required for all its geographic locations[15]. From this point of view, the geographic locations[16] suffering from a lack of freedoms PL^j are those that have not yet reached L^i_0, but a lower level of L_0 for each location j: $PL^j = L^i_0 - L_0$. From this abstract point of view, there also exists a minimal level of information and communication IC^i_0, consistent with the minimum freedoms attained by a society L^i_0. In addition, there should be a minimum capability level CAP^i_0, consistent with the

---

[14] Disincentives refer to problems of: unsuitability and obsolescence; existence of a process of creative destruction; need of technological substitution and reorganization of the productive activity; creation of winners and losers, and resistance from the latter; attitude of the society towards the innovations within a democratic environment; shortage of factors complementary to new technologies; uncertainty of the technological direction of the future, and its economic result; attraction of new innovations towards geographical concentrations.

[15] From here on, the location is taken as the unit of analysis, since universal access will continue to be the main goal to achieve in the middle term in most of the countries in Latin America.

[16] From here on, poor geographic locations will be understood as rural locations with fewer than 1000 inhabitants (it could be considered even with fewer than 5000 inhabitants), based on observations made in Latin America. Poor neighborhoods in urban areas are not included, since they pose a different problem, one of universal service, where the household is the unit of analysis.

minimum level of information and communication IC^i_0. Access to information may be instrumental for identifying a person's desired demand of freedoms. Usually, the poorer are not aware of the opportunities available for improving their standard of living. In this sense, the minimum capabilities of information and communication also play a 'catalytic' role for the advancement of the freedoms in other aspects of the life of the poor. Therefore, we arrive at the definition of information and communication poverty ICP^j, as the deprivation of basic capabilities to participate in the information society:

$$ICP^j = CAP^i_0 - CAP^{ij}_0 \quad (1)$$

The minimum capabilities CAP^i_0 define the information and communication poverty line, and the observed capabilities CAP^{ij}_0 for each geographic location j establish the distance to the poverty line.

This poverty line implies the minimum capability required to participate in the information society, which has three components summarized in Table 1. The geographic location must have a set of minimum assets related to ICT, basic health care and education, social capital and productive capability. It should be able to exchange (receive and provide) a minimum of transparent information about political, institutional, economic processes (including those of production, commercialization and income distribution), and about social protection mechanisms. It must be able to communicate, through the analysis and a minimum level of exchange of ideas about political, institutional, technological and economic processes as well as social protection mechanisms[17]. In addition, the three-component set of minimum capabilities to own assets and exchange information and communication must be consistent with each other[18].

---

[17] This approach is also consistent with a phenomenon examined by the literature on poverty, which refers to the relationship between the ability to obtain income and the ability to use such income (Sen, 1995). In our case, one issue is the problem resulting from inequalities and a lack of basic capabilities to participate in the information society, and another issue, though related, is the problem caused by inequalities which prevent transforming such participation in the information society into new capabilities.

[18] Another way of understanding the difference between exchange of information and exchange of ideas is the difference between stock of knowledge and increase of such stock.

Table 1: **Guidelines on Required Interrelated Capabilities**

ASSETS	INFORMATION	COMMUNICATION
Ownership and capability to use:	Capability to exchange transparent information about:	Capability to analyze and exchange ideas about:
Physical assets: ICT	Political processes and their outcomes	Political processes
Human assets: Health care and education essential for ICT	Institutional processes and their outcomes	Institutional and organizational designs
Social assets: Social networks for ICT	Social protection mechanisms and their outcomes	Control and evaluation of transparency
Economic assets: Productive uses of ICT	Technology and processes of information management for the improvement of production, commercialization and a more transparent income distribution	Social protection mechanisms
		Technology, productive processes, and exchange and distribution

According to this approach, it is not possible to identify the poverty line under a single criterion. It is necessary to consider several criteria at the same time to generate a global indicator. Individual and aggregate indicators published by the World Economic Forum (2004) and by Orbicom (2003) are examples. However, such indicators are characterized by their bias towards indicators that only measure the accumulation of assets[19], corresponding to the first column of Table 1. On the other hand, the capabilities approach goes beyond the accumulation of assets. In order to obtain information exchange capabilities, training and experiences in generating and using information on the topics listed in the second column of Table 1 are required. To obtain capabilities to exchange ideas, training and experiences in the creation and use of innovations on the topics listed in the third column of Table 1 are required.

How is it possible to obtain the minimum global indicator that represents the poverty line? In practical terms, the identification of a reference location for the country or geographical zone under analysis is recommended. This geographic location is characterized by participating in the information society, regardless of having the lowest possible set of indicators; in other words, it represents the poverty line location. The selection of such a geographic location would be arbitrary, as there will be different interpretations regarding the meaning of participation in the information society and the meaning of minimum indicators[20] for a specific location. This

[19] Physical, human and environmental assets of business, government and not poor individuals, indicated by country, in the case of the World Economic Forum. Physical and human assets and the intensity of its use, indicated by country, in the case of Orbicom. Even though the latter includes an interesting discussion on the need of knowledge and capabilities to understand and use the available information. Several of these ideas are included in Table 2.

[20] The poverty line location might be an observable or an abstract location.

extent of arbitrariness is similar to the one frequently observed in the definition of access or universal service goals. As Cherry and Wildman (1999) point out, this is a consequence of the fact that the goal definition is the product of a socio-political process, which responds to a specific set of temporary economic and technological possibilities. In our case, the poverty line location reflects the goal of universal access to the information society; a goal that must be defined through a participative political process. This last point is particularly relevant since societies will express their concerns about what the real priorities for poverty reduction are. For instance, the issue will come up whether or not efforts should first concentrate on health care, education, and basic services or on the access to new information and communication technologies. Literature on participatory processes (Chambers 1997; Nelson and Wright, 1995) highlights a methodology of participation, and the implications these processes have on power relationships between the dominant class and the excluded and poor sectors of a society. In the context of information poverty, it is necessary to highlight that the poor have to identify, through a collaborative process, the opportunities and challenges that ICT can offer to improve their standard of living, i.e. the access to basic services as education and health care.

3.2. AGGREGATE MEASUREMENT OF POVERTY

The purpose of choosing a poverty line location is to measure the distance from other locations to that reference line. This implies that individual and global indicators must be generated for every location studied. A foreseeable problem is the array of characteristics and differences among locations and their environment, which would not allow for a comparison among them. A natural solution to this problem is the monetary appreciation of distances, by calculating the economic cost of achieving the goal of universal access to the information society for each location j: EC^j. The economic cost refers to the investment of assets and to the operational expenditure in information exchanges and communications required to reach the poverty line location. The advantage of converting the indicators into economic costs of access for each location is that the estimate of such costs forces us to consider geographical differences of distinct locations. That is, the economic cost of access would equal the global indicator of capabilities, adjusted by the differences, and it would also be more accurate[21], permitting the desired aggregation.

---

[21] In Sen's own words, for the relationship between income and capabilities, we have come to the following conclusion (Nussbaum and Sen, 1996, pg.69): "Therefore, the most accurate characterization of poverty as a lack of basic capabilities, from the point of view of the cause, can also be made in the most traditional format based on adequate income. The difference in the formulation is not relevant. What matters is to take note of the interpersonal and intersectorial variations between income and capabilities. This is the special contribution of the capability approach in the analysis of poverty."

The following equation summarizes the measurement of the information and communication poverty:

$$EC^j = F\ (CAP^i_0,\ LC^j,\ TC^j,\ UC^j)\quad (2)$$

Where:

EC^j = Economic cost of location j to reach the poverty line location. It includes the cost of investment in assets and the operational expenditure in exchange of information and ideas.

CAP^i_0 = Minimum capabilities that define the poverty line location, consistent with equation (1). It includes the indicators for ownership and capability to use assets, and the indicators for capabilities of exchange of information and ideas.

LC^j = Local Constraints of location j. It is the set of characteristics of location j based on structural restrictions that hinder its access to the information society.

TC^j = Technological Constraints of location j. It is the set of characteristics that determine the space of possible technological solutions, given the state of local technology and infrastructure.

UC^j = ICT Usage Constraints of location j. It is the set of characteristics unique to ICT management, given the local capabilities.

F = Function that transforms the characteristics of the poverty line location dependent on local, technology and usage restrictions into economic costs.

With the economic cost of access for each location, and provided that the economic cost of the poverty line location is zero, the aggregated measurements of the information and communication poverty can be calculated and its magnitude and depth can be identified. Existing methods such as those of Foster-Greer-Thorbecke (FGT) and Sen-Shorrocks-Thon (SST) can be used, the only difference being that they would be applied to geographic locations instead of households.

3.3. CURRENT LOCAL CAPABILITIES (CAP)

Understanding the current information and communication capabilities (initial situation) of each location under study would allow us to identify which would be considered by society as the poverty line location. In addition, it would let us identify the "distance" from the other location to the poverty line location in order to estimate the cost of reaching it. Which information, consistent with Table 1, should be required for this purpose? Table 2 shows a summary of this information, including basic capabilities to use physical, human, economic and social assets and the capability to exchange information and ideas which shall significantly affect the required economic cost to

Table 2: **Current State of Information and Communication Capabilities by Location**

Ownership and Capability to Use Assets				Capability of Information and Communication Exchange	
Physical Assets	Human Assets	Social Assets	Economic Assets	Experience in Information Exchange (EIE)	Experience in Ideas Exchange or Communication (EIC)
Public telephones /100 inhab.	% of ICT literacy, in Males and Females	Indicators of social networks of information exchange	Indicators of ICT use within productive chain for the improvement of production, commercialization and income distribution	Number of individuals with EIE in political processes/100 inhab.*	Number of people with EIC in political processes/100 inhab.*
VF Radios/100 inhab.	% of Males and Females with only primary education and ICT use. Years	Indicators of a collaborative culture and conflict resolution	% of companies and production units that use ICT	Number of people with EIE in institutional processes/100 inhab.*	Number of people with EIC in institutional processes/100 inhab.*
% of households with ICT	% of M and F with secondary education and ICT use. Years	Confidence and reciprocity indicators	Number of new business contacts obtained through ICT	Number of people with EIE in productive processes/100 inhab.*	Number of people with EIC in productive processes/100 inhab.*
Do schools have ICT? Are they accessible to the public?	% of M and F with vocational school and ICT use. Years	Indicators of representation and political participation	% of sales through e-business	Number of people with EIE in social protection/100 inhab.*	Number of people with EIC in social protection/100 inhab.*
Do health centers have ICT? Are they accessible to the public?	Number of experts and professionals and ICT use. Which professions?	Indicators of the cultural view of information and communication exchange	% of income increase thanks to the reduction of i) transaction costs, ii) transportation costs, and iii) time costs obtained through ICT	Training centers for information exchange. Indicators of access to such centers	Training centers for the information exchange. Indicators of access to such centers
Do government offices have ICT? Are they accessible to the public?	Age structure and gender of those who use ICT. What is the use given to ICT? Why?	Do social organizations have ICT? Are they accessible to the public?	Indicators of employment based on ICT (software, telecenters, resale services)	Indicators of capability to identify transparency differences in the information	Social spaces for the exchange of ideas and debate. Characteristics of such spaces
Do production units have ICT? Are they accessible to the public?	ICT and languages used by population /100 inhab.	Traditional local knowledge In which areas? And in which ways?		Household expenditure on training related to information exchange	Indicators of action capabilities and decision-making processes. Level of autonomy and interference
Distance to nearest location with required ICT? What's the transportation cost?	Household monthly expenditure in ICT by unit of consumption	Protection of rights about traditional local knowledge		Experience in publication and diffusion of information and ideas	Capabilities to create incentives to disclose transparent information
	What are the uses given to ICT?				Capability to put knowledge into and out of context
	Number of households with children studying outside the location				Capability to integrate local knowledge with other kinds of knowledge
					Household expenditure on training related to the exchange of ideas and knowledge
					Capability to cooperate, exchange, and coordinate with other people out of the location/country
					Capability to establish alliances and networks with outsiders

ICT = Radio, TV, Cable TV, fixed telephone, mobile telephone, computer, Internet.

(*) Including number of years of experience and training on a specific subject.

reach the poverty line location. This exchange of information and ideas must be transparent, contrary to asymmetrical information. The latter increases transaction costs, uncertainty, risk, and legal costs, resulting in suboptimal decisions for the economic agents. It is the opposite of having the information disclosed and provided in the amount and quality required, flowing without limitations. New ICT, in the framework of the construction of the information society, may contribute to reducing information costs and the asymmetry of information. ICT would not only have impact on production, consumption and exchange, but also on social, cultural and political aspects.

3.4. LOCAL CONSTRAINTS (LC)

Local structural restrictions are a group of economic, demographic, social and geographical characteristics that determine rural poverty and its reproduction, as shown

Table 3: **Local Structural Constraints**

Economic Characteristics	Demographic Characteristics	Social Characteristics	Geographic Characteristics
Level of extreme poverty which represents a great restriction for payment capacity	Population size and density	Health and access to health services	Geographical, weather and environmental characteristics
Access to production	Fertility and mortality rates	Education and access to educational services	Level of geographical isolation
Basic services (electricity and water)	Population structure by age and gender	Availability of rules and internal and external social networks	Availability and quality of roads
Quality of employment and rate of unemployment	Migratory characteristics	Ability of self help and cooperation	Availability and quality of transportation means
Structure of household income	Registered and documented population	Indicators of social mobility	Usual means of transport
Structure of household expenditure	Mother language and most spoken languages	Number of schools, up to which grade	Distance and time of transport to markets, health, educational, and management centers
Ownership and productivity of assets	Number and size of households	Number of health centers, and services offered	
Basic services of electricity, water, gas, housing quality and equipment	Responsible members of the household	Indicators of local rules, of legal and civic protection	
Production destined to self-consumption, to internal and external markets	Literacy rate, school attendance, educational level, years of study	Number of social organizations; activities and characteristics	
Economic, gender and ethnic inequalities	Handicapped population		
Government offices and services offered			
Number of production units; activities and characteristics			

in Table 3. These restrictions may be mitigated by the benefits of access to the information society.

3.5. USAGE CONSTRAINTS (UC)

Structural usage constraints are a group of internal factors of ICT, related to connectivity, content, training, and sustainability, as shown in Table 4.

Table 4: **Structural Constraints to ICT Use**

Connectivity	Content	Training	Sustainability
High connectivity costs High costs of Internet use in rural areas Problems of equipment installation Problems of equipment and software maintenance	Lack of local and relevant contents Academic level of the content, with little applicability to the reality of the poor Language problems (high percentage of content in English)	Lack of human capability to use ICT Literacy is a requirement for use Permanent changes in software requires continuous training Tools' design is based on the needs of urban users	Need of a users' network (scale effects of investment in infrastructure) Need of human capability for the proper management of ICT

3.6. TECHNOLOGICAL CONSTRAINTS (TC)

Technology has peculiar characteristics that may mean restrictions or opportunities, depending on the incentives or disincentives generated for the demand and supply, as shown in Table 5.

Table 5: **Technological Opportunities and Constraints**

Demand's point of view	Supply's point of view
Economies of strategic complementarity, compatibility and standards, consumption external factors and substitution and lock-in costs, typical of markets characterized by network economies (Shy, 2001; Shapiro and Varian, 1999). In many cases, it implies very high and continuous costs for developing countries. Strategies of discrimination due to delay in dissemination of information, quality discrimination, production of new versions, renting before sale and production of different versions (Shy, 2001). Coexistence, flexibility and technological convergence that allow for a variety of technological solutions, for every need and circumstance. This is an opportunity. Adaptation of problems of technologies designed for developed countries to the realities of developing countries.	Production conditions characterized by scale economies. High level of technological innovation on data transmission and technological convergence demand continuous and significant investments. High fixed and sunk costs of information production, and at the same time, additional costs of reproduction and distribution almost null. Competition limited to few operators can give rise to the exercise of market power. It favors the operator.

4. Conclusions and Some Implications

From the methodological point of view, the poverty line location approach to the measurement of information and communication poverty introduced in this paper departs from mainstream international development practice in three aspects. Firstly, the pro-poor approach is treated as a priority compared to the pro-competitiveness approach. Secondly, comparisons are made between different locations in the same country, instead of comparisons between countries. This contributes to identifying the problem more accurately inside each country in order to design public policies according to the country's own realities and restrictions. Thirdly, the economic cost is measured to reach the poverty line location. This offers more accurate information for drafting public policy, which goes beyond the mere presentation of connectivity and usage indicators.

In conceptual terms, the approach of information and communication poverty contributes to the understanding that information and communication are essential for the advancement of human freedoms. Thus, besides the need to strengthen the poor's capabilities for the ownership and use of economic assets, there are new capabilities for the exchange of information and ideas about the economy, politics and society.

This approach also emphasizes that information and communication are a variable included in a group of interdependent variables related to the general issue of poverty. The success of achieving the minimum capability to participate in the information society depends on and, at the same time, affects other critical aspects of poverty such as education, health care, social networks, productivity and political participation.

Another important issue resulting from this approach is the need to acknowledge structural restrictions. Many restrictions act against, and others favor the adoption of new information and communication capabilities. However, the adoption contributes, at the same time, to mitigating the negative structural restrictions.

From the point of view of public policy, the information and communication poverty measurement carried out by the establishment of a poverty line location introduces the need to consider three new issues. First, it opens the discussion on what the poverty line location should be according to the realities of a society. Second, it informs on the magnitude and depth of such poverty, location by location, and aggregately, by indicators translated into the economic cost of reducing poverty. Third, it necessarily opens the discussion on the identification of incentives and restrictions (financial, institutional, organizational and technological) for a real participation by rural communities, markets and governments in a policy design to reduce the information and communication poverty.

Figure 1: **Information and Communication Poverty Approach**

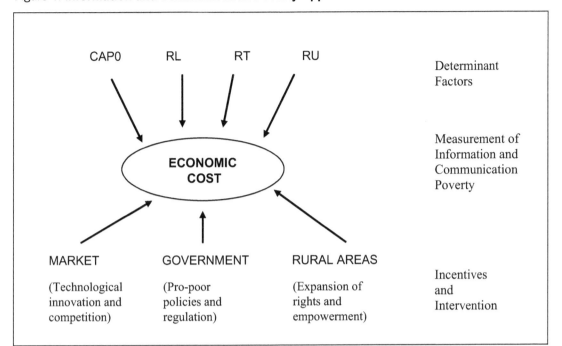

In terms of incentives and restrictions for participation by households and organizations in rural communities, the self help and empowerment level depend on practical outcomes of the information and communication exchange over the reduction of structural restrictions and the release of new capabilities.

In terms of incentives and restrictions for the market's participation – despite the great advances in technological innovations, reduction of costs, competition and coverage, as well as the advances in regulation – the performance of the market and the private telecommunications and information supply tend to divide the population by two: those who have a willingness to pay equal or higher prices than the market's price and those who have a willingness to pay a lower price. The market also tends to divide the population into two geographical areas; market coverage is reduced to urban areas and rural locations where investment can be profitably recovered. A free market will not supply the service in urban areas and rural locations where profitability cannot be ensured. This consequence causes concern, particularly in countries with low levels of economic and human development and a high level of social inequality, typical of Latin American societies, where an important part of the population has low willingness to pay and lives in not-profitable urban areas or rural locations.

In terms of incentives and restrictions to participation by the government the acknowledgment that participation in the information society is a public good and the prospects that the social benefits are higher than social costs usually contribute to justify government intervention through pro-poor policies specifically targeted at reducing the information and communication poverty. In practice, implemented policies have typically been called policies of universal access/service aiming at extending the coverage of telecommunication services beyond the market. These policies generally include private participation, based on subsidies to investment and, in some cases, on subsidies to operations. Universal access via subsidies is possible. Diverse technological solutions can be designed as well as geographical areas of concession identified by merging profitable and non profitable locations in order to minimize subsidies. Not all countries have achieved the implementation of universal access programs as they are very demanding in terms of institutional and organizational ability, in addition to financial restrictions. When national government programs fail, non governmental solutions arise. They are usually more flexible and effective, although they may also be more expensive (duplication of efforts, errors, and investments), isolated, and of limited impact.

References

Attanasio, O. & Székely, M. (1999). *An Asset-Based Approach to the Analysis of Poverty in Latin America*. Mimeo.

Bourguignon, F. (2000). *The Pace of Economic Growth and Poverty Reduction*. Paris: The World Bank and Delta. Mimeo.

Chambers, R. (1997a). *Whose Reality Counts: Putting the Last First*. London: Intermediate Technology Publications.

Cherry, B.A. & Wildman, S. (1999). Conceptualizing Universal Service: Definitions, context, social process and politics. In Cherry, B.A., Wildman, S. and Hammond, A. (Editors). *Making Universal Service Policy: Enhancing the Process through a Multidisciplinary Evaluation*. Mahwah: Lawrence Erlbaum Associates Publishers.

Dollar, D. & Kraay, A. (2000). *Growth is Good for the Poor*. Development Research Group. The World Bank. Mimeo.

Easterly, W. (2003). *Search of Growth: Wanderings and Tribulations of Development Economists*. Spanish Edition. Barcelona: Antoni Bosch.

Foster, J., Greer, J. & Thorbecke, E. (1984). A Class of Decomposable Poverty Measures. *Econometrica*, 52 (3), 761-766.

Gigler, B.S. (2001). Empowerment through the Internet: Opportunities and Challenges for Indigenous Peoples. In: Technology for Social Action. *TechKnowLogia, July/August*.

Gigler, B.S. (2005). Enacting and interpreting technology from usage to well-being: Experiences of indigenous peoples with ICT. In Rahman, H., *Empowering Marginal Communities with Information Networking*. Idea Group.

Kenny, C. (2003). Development's False Divide – Giving Internet Access to the World's Poorest Will Cost a Lot and Accomplish Little. *Foreign Policy, Jan.-Feb.*, 76-77.

Lora, E., Pagés, C., Panizza, U. & Stein, E. (2004). *A Decade of Development Thinking*. Research Department. Washington, D.C.: Inter-American Development Bank.

McNamara, K.S. (2000). Why Wired? The Importance of Access to Information and Communication Technologies. *International Journal of Technologies for the Advance of Knowledge and Learning, March/April*.

McNamara, K.S. (2003). Information and Communication Technologies, *Poverty and Development: Learning from Experience*. A Background paper for the InfoDev Annual Symposium. Washington, D.C.: The World Bank.

Nelson, N. & Wright, S. (1995). Participation and Power, in: Nelson and Wright (Editors). *Power and Participatory Practice*. London: IT.

Orbicom. (2003). *Monitoring the Digital Divide and Beyond*. Sciadas, G. (Editor). Claude-Yves Charron Publisher. Ottawa: NRC Press.

Ravallion, M. (2000). *Growth and Poverty: Making Sense of the Current Debate*. Mimeo. Washington DC: The World Bank.

Robeyns, I. (2004). *Assessing Global Poverty and Inequality: Income, Resources and Capabilities*. Preprint Article. Metaphilosophy LLC and Blackwell Publishers.

Sen, A. (1995). Markets and Freedoms: Achievements and Limitations of the Market Mechanism in Promoting Individual Freedoms. In *New Welfare Economy Selected Writing*. Valencia: University of Valencia.

Sen, A. (1996). *Capability and Welfare in the Quality of Life*. Nussbaum, M. & Sen, A. (Compilers). Spanish Edition. Mexico: Fondo de Cultura Económica.

Sen, A. (2000). *Development and Freedom.* Spanish Edition. Argentina: Editorial Planeta.

Shapiro, C. & Varian, H. (1999). *The Information Domain: A Strategic Guide for Network Economics.* Spanish Edition. Barcelona: Antoni Bosh.

Shy, O. (2001). *The Economics of Networks Industries.* Cambridge, UK: Cambridge University Press.

Székely, M. (2001). *Where to from here? Generating Capabilities and Creating Opportunities for the Poor.* Research Network Working paper R-431. Washington, D.C.: Inter-American Development Bank.

World Bank Institute. (2005). *Poverty Manual.* [Electronic Version]. The World Bank Group.

World Economic Forum. (2004). *Global Information Technology Report 2003-2004.*

CHAPTER 2

Analysis of ICT Demand: What Is Digital Poverty and How to Measure It?

Roxana Barrantes [1]
INSTITUTO DE ESTUDIOS PERUANOS

Abstract

This chapter discusses the notions of poverty, information needs and information and communication technologies (ICT) to offer a concept of digital poverty and estimate the digital poverty level in Latin America and the Caribbean. The chapter is composed of two sections. The first section contains the conceptual discussion of digital poverty, its types and possible levels. ICT are defined based on their use and the conditions for such use. Digital poverty is therefore defined as a lack of ICT and might be a feature of any population segment, whether or not economically poor. In the second section of this chapter the concept of digital poverty and its resulting classifications are validated by using data from a household survey (ENAHO) carried out in Peru. Lastly, the conclusions and future research lines are presented.

[1] This research was developed at the Institute of Peruvian Studies, as part of the institutional activities on the development of the Information Society. The research is part of the first stage of the Regional Dialogue on the Information Society (REDIS-DIRSI). Comments by Ramón Díaz, Natalia González, Carmen Montero and Carolina Trivelli, IEP members, and by Leonardo Mena and Jorge Dussan from REDIS-DIRSI, contributed to this paper. We acknowledge Tilsa Oré Mónago for her research assistance. Errors and omissions are my responsibility.

1. Introduction

This paper is the first step of a more comprehensive study, which intends to analyze the demand for Information and Communication Technologies (ICT) to design policies aimed at obtaining a more effective growth in access and fostering successful efforts to increase coverage and a productive use of ICT. It is developed as one of the works included in the Regional Dialogue on the Information Society (REDIS-DIRSI), which gathers researchers from Latin America and the Caribbean (LAC), under the coordination of the Institute for Connectivity in the Americas (ICA-IDRC). This work is part of a larger effort to design regulatory and public policies to increase ICT access by the region's marginalized sectors.

Demand analysis cannot be separated from digital poverty. Economics tells us that only those people with enough buying power can be part of the goods/services demand, and that this will happen only when the benefits of such good or service are known. Demand is therefore restricted by two main factors: the lack of income and the lack of information regarding the benefit associated with the consumption of the good/service.

Several topics need to be defined and discussed when posing this issue. Some of them are issues related to an economic understanding of demand, which requires resorting to traditional economic theories – briefly revised in this paper – to set a framework for the subsequent discussion. This review requires a definition of the product demanded; thus, a definition of ICT is also pertinent to this analysis.

Considering the issue from the perspective of ICT demand, we must undertake an in depth study of one of the key factors of market demand for the service: income levels and their distribution. The approach allows us to extend the discussion to the relationship between poverty and ICT, towards a concept that has not been sufficiently discussed: "digital poverty" – the lack of goods and services based on ICT.

This lack of goods and services can at the same time be analyzed from two different perspectives. One is ICT demand by the marginalized sectors, and digital poverty measures, or low income/economically poor people's lack of ICT. This is the most common point of view (Nyaka, 2002) and leads us to study the role played by ICT in overcoming economic poverty, including the traditionally marginalized sectors.

However, from another perspective, it is relevant to analyze how much the demand for the service is affected by a set of joint or sequential consumption variables, which define "digital illiteracy"[2] or digital poverty, as we will refer to it in this chapter. This is an aspect of measuring digital poverty at the general population level, which includes paying attention to all individuals who, for different reasons, neither use nor demand ICT.

---

[2] ETS (2002).

At this point, we decided to apply the conceptual framework proposed. We used the National Survey of Living Standards in Peru (ENAHO), which allowed us to focus on one ICT aspect – connectivity –, based on data obtained from households, not individuals.

This chapter is organized in two parts. The first part includes basic concepts such as demand, poverty and information needs to define the concept of digital poverty. The application of the conceptual framework is included in the second part of this chapter, and shows interesting results, despite database limitations such as measuring household aspects and a single feature of digital poverty. This chapter ends with conclusions and research areas for further study.

2. Economic Concept of Demand[3]

Demand, as understood by economists, is defined as the amount of a good/service people are willing to buy at a certain price. Demand is therefore a concept affected by buying power – without it, a person may have needs but not demand. Buying power is, in turn, affected by the consumer's income. With insufficient income, demand can be null or reduced, even if the need is urgent.

Demand or buying power for a good/service arises from the consumer's preferences for specific goods. Thus, two issues become relevant in the analysis: defining a good and studying how the consumer orders his/her preferences for such good in relation to other available goods.

The definition of a good plays a vital role when establishing consumer preferences. Defining a good means knowing it, knowing its use, and the disadvantages (or costs) associated with its consumption; that means knowing the full benefits of its consumption. Defining a good means to define the group of attributes or features of such a good that fulfill a consumer's need. Demand arises, then, from a previous knowledge of the good and a subjective evaluation of its advantages (benefits) and disadvantages (costs).

Those who do not know the good/service or who do not have the necessary buying power will not have demand. Hence the importance of advertising when introducing new products. We might enter a vicious circle: the most excluded within marginalized sectors, those with no access to information, will never have demand, because they will never know the benefits of the service.

The theory of consumer demand leads us to pose several questions regarding our research, among which we would like to mention only three. A first question refers to the definition of ICT: what they are, what type of good they are, the set of attributes

---

[3] Concepts discussed within this section are part of an introduction to economic theory course, for which ample bibliography is available. Among a wide variety of references, I cite Varian (2002).

that can be associated with ICT, and the possibility of identifying a hierarchical order within this set. An additional question will explore the income level needed for ICT demand. Finally, the concept of digital poverty is discussed, with regards to the lack of ICT.

3. Service Definition: Information, Communication and ICT

In order to talk about digital poverty, we will first discuss digital media for information and communication, known as "Information and Communication Technologies" or ICT.[4] This essay will discuss this definition based on a variety of attributes associated with ICT use and consumption.

- **Connectivity.** A means of communication is necessary. This includes end user equipment and fixed or wireless networks. These will meet connectivity needs for radio receivers, television devices, fixed or mobile telephone services, and computers, which will be supported by the capacity to transmit information, be it content (broadband vs. fixed phone voice lines) or distance (television or radio).

- **Communication.** It may be one-way or two-way communication. This defines the type of connectivity and the usage of the information involved. For instance, television gives information but does not allow for information exchange, unless another means is used.

- **Information.** At the same time, information is divided into creation, storage, broadcasting, exchange and consumption. It is important to note that information has both private and public components. As a public good, information – once available – generates benefits that are not exclusive; that is why we tend to make less information available than would be efficient.

In this chapter, ICT demand will be understood as the demand for these attributes, which may be fulfilled through the consumption of all goods and services having such attributes, or through the consumption of a subcategory of such products. The demand for ICT reflects the demand for the information and communication they offer. Therefore, they simply mediate the human need for information and communication.

---

[4] For ICT definitions, please check World Bank (2002), Nayki (2002), or Orbicom (2003), among many other references.

4. Conceptual Framework of Digital Poverty

The concept of "digital poverty" does not frequently appear to be mentioned in discussions[5]. "Digital divide" is the most frequently used concept, generally understood as measuring the inequalities in ICT access and in the use of ICT at the household or country levels[6]. Contrary to the concept of the digital divide, the digital poverty concept tries to find the minimum ICT use and consumption levels, as well as the income levels of the population necessary to demand ICT products.

When introducing the concept of digital poverty, we are stating that the concern is not focused on any type of information or communication, but on the data that can be stored, made available, used and consumed by digital media. Hence, we are introducing a specific dimension: the use of computers or digital communication technologies that broaden the equipment's functionality, such as mobile phones, in order to facilitate information and communication.

In this approach, digitally poor individuals lack the information and communications enabled by digital technologies due to a lack of knowledge on how they are used, or a lack of income – demand considerations. Technologies are the means but, at the same time, their availability is the most visible component of the demand that can be estimated.

Therefore, digitally poor individuals are not only low-income persons or people with unfulfilled basic needs, with no access to ICT nor usage of them; digitally poor individuals may also include people who, otherwise, could not be called poor. Thus, there are several types of digitally poor people:

- Low income or economically poor individuals, who do not have the minimum abilities required to use ICT and to whom services are not offered. There is a double restriction for ICT use: supply and ability restrictions.

- Low income or economically poor individuals with no service available, although they have the minimum abilities required to use ICT. There is only a supply restriction for ICT use.

- Economically poor individuals who do not demand, although they have the minimum abilities required to use ICT. It is precisely their lack of income that does not allow them to take part in ICT demand. There is a demand restriction for ICT use.

- Individuals who are not economically poor but have no demand because they do not have the minimum abilities required. This poverty appears more clearly as a generational gap.

---

[5] A simple search in Google of the phrase had no hits for those words combined in Spanish, and only one reference in English, related to the "digital divide". Search conducted on May 14th, 2005.

[6] Please see Orbicom (2003), ALADI (2003), NTIA (1999) and UIT (2003).

Taking into account this approach, marginalized sectors with low income levels are not the only digitally poor individuals. Digitally poor individuals may be those who do not use ICT due to lack of services provided or to the lack of ability to use them.

Our discussion states that digital poverty can be studied from two different perspectives:

1. The traditional approach, as we call it, which analyzes ICT access of low income individuals or economically poor people with unfulfilled basic needs. Economically poor individuals may be digitally poor people due to supply or demand characteristics:

    a. If it is a supply problem, we will try to identify economically poor people who lack connectivity. This is the most studied problem in the literature, which focuses on how to eradicate the connectivity or digital divide, and which aims at making transmission means, telephones, computers and Internet connections available to population centers.

    b. If it is a demand problem, we will try to identify the economically poor individuals having supply sources. This will basically be an urban problem, as cities in our countries have supply sources such as telecenters, and therefore it is not necessary to have a computer in every household. The issue of public policy lies in how to broaden the use of ICT.

2. An approach that studies the lack of ICT, or the lack of ICT literacy. This concept of literacy would be equivalent to the inability to read and write and, in absence of a better term, "ICT illiterate" could be used. This lack may be a characteristic of both the economically and non-economically poor people. In the case of economically poor people, an ICT illiterate individual will clearly be illiterate, with no exposure to modern electrical appliances or to cable television; someone without an immigrant relative to be in contact with. Nevertheless, an ICT illiterate individual can be a person whose needs are completely fulfilled, as is the case of an elderly person whose daily activities do not expose or require him/her to be familiar with computers, appliances or modern technology in general.

We will then use four variables to define digitally poor individuals:

1. **Age.** The hypothesis states that the older the person, the higher the likelihood that he/she will be a digitally poor person. It is a way of measuring human capital.

2. **Education.** The hypothesis states that the higher the educational level, the less likely it is that he/she will be a digitally poor person. It is the most common way of measuring human capital.

3. **Available Infrastructure.** Radio, open television, fixed and mobile telephone services, cable television, computers, and Internet access are taken into account.

4. **Functionality Accomplished.** Functionality refers to the uses given to technology: from the mere reception of information to the full interaction involved in electronic government procedures or purchases, as well as the creation of contents.

It is possible to suggest the classification of digital poverty or digital wealth observed in Table 1, where the above types of digitally poor people are related to the different ICT attributes: the higher the level of connectivity, the lower the level of digital poverty. We have identified four levels, classified from 0 to III.

Table 1: **Digital Poverty**

Connectivity Level	Functionality	Infrastructure	Educational Level	Age
III.	Digital Interaction (Electronic Government and Business)	Internet Broadband	High	Youths
II.	Electronic Messaging	Internet / Mobile Telephone Services	Middle	Young and Not-So-Young People
I.	Communication and Reception of Information	Telephone Services (Fixed or Mobile)	Low But Not Illiterate	Elderly
0	Reception of Information	Radio or Television	Illiterate	Elderly

Extremely digitally poor people are, according to this diagram, those with a digital connectivity level equal to 0. The extremely digitally poor person will typically be someone who uses technology for the reception of information. This may be due to lack of knowledge of ICT use or lack of communication services. However, even when services are available, the person's age and learning ability may hinder his/her knowledge to fully use the equipment.

Digitally poor people have a connectivity level equal to I. Digitally poor people have communication media available, so they can receive information and can communicate. However, the use of digital media is limited due to a lack of supply or of human capital, a low educational level, a high degree of illiteracy or older age.

Those individuals with connectivity levels II and III are not digitally poor people. In these cases, there is Internet access, but the difference between the two groups is the functionality of their Internet access. At level II, there is a passive use, whereas at level III, active use is observed, since the individuals in this group have the knowledge needed to make transactions or to take advantage of electronic government applications.

Taxonomy cannot be rigid if it intends to be useful. Two variables allow for a more flexible taxonomy: age and economic poverty. On the one hand, the economically poor, young people living in areas with no connection (supply problem) will not belong to level III. On the other hand, it will be difficult to classify elderly people, even if they are not poor, in level III.

This discussion can be summarized in the following figure, which introduces some considerations taken into account when classifying variables related to human capital, by using the arrows located at the right. People show greater digital wealth the higher their educational level, and lower digital wealth the higher their age.

Figure 1: **Digital Poverty Level**

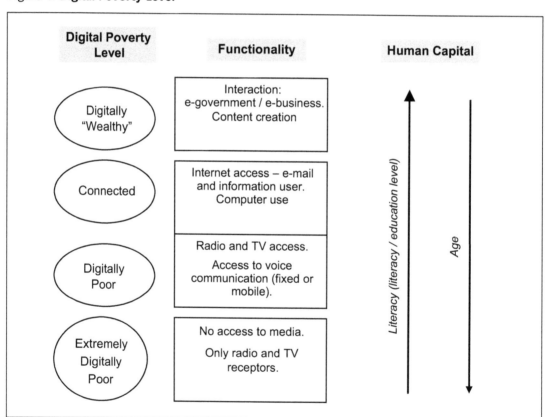

The approach used for measuring digital poverty has more similarities with the one used for estimating unfulfilled basic needs than with the one used to find the deficit when purchasing a basic family food basket. Therefore, an individual who does not fulfill his/her communication and information needs through digital means will be considered an extremely digitally poor person.

The approach presented in the conceptual framework requires researching ICT use in order to determine not only the connectivity component, which is the most studied one, but also the connectivity use. In other words, if ICT demand is understood as a demand for connectivity attributes, information consumption, and information and communication availability, the measurement of digital poverty should estimate the dimensions of each attribute for every individual, and determine the person's lack in each aspect.

5. A Measurement Exercise of Digital Poverty

In order to illustrate the possible applications of this conceptual framework, we use the Peruvian National Survey of Living Standards (ENAHO) of 2003. It should be noted that ENAHO gathers socioeconomic household information, while the conceptual framework proposed can only be applied to individuals, since not only access, but the type of Internet usage is important to determine a certain individual's placement within the gradient of digital poverty. Therefore, the outcomes of this exercise are merely illustrative of the type of analysis enabled by the conceptual framework, as we can only observe the ICT connectivity attribute, but not the reception/broadcasting attributes of information and/or communication.

After clarifying that point, let us examine the results obtained. For the classification we will only select households with complete answers regarding having and accessing ICT, a total of 17,680 households. This universe will be known as a "selected sample." We think it advisable to describe the household groups according to their poverty level. The total sample, as well as the selected one, were classified according to the poverty level by expenditure deficit. Classification outcomes are shown in Table 2. The selected sample reproduces poverty results found at the national level: about 48% of the households qualify as poor households, and 18% of the households in the nation are considered extremely poor households, since they do not have the resources to purchase a family basic food basket.

Table 2: **Poverty in Peruvian Households**

Poverty Level	Selected Sample		Total Sample of ENAHO	
	Nº. Obs.	(%)	Nº. Obs.	(%)
Extremely Poor	3 328	18.82	3 424	18.1
Not Extremely Poor	5 024	28.42	5 158	27.27
Not Poor	9 328	52.76	10 330	54.62
Total	17 680	100	18 912	100

Source: ENAHO 2003

We then classified the selected sample households depending on their digital poverty level, only according to the connectivity attribute discussed in the previous section. The extremely digitally poor households are those that neither have access to voice communication nor to the Internet in telecenters. Digitally poor people do not have access to the Internet but do have access to voice communications. Connected people have Internet access only in telecenters, and digitally wealthy people are those who have Internet access in the household and own a personal computer.

When applying the instrument, we found that the strict application of the criteria could make us lose sight of an important group of households[7]. In particular, the conceptual framework proposes a classification with increasing connectivity and ICT use, but Peruvian households show more Internet access in telecenters than phone use. Therefore, if the connected people group had included only those who have a telephone but access the Internet only in telecenters, we would have missed the information of more than 10% of the households participating in the survey, which have Internet access in telecenters but do not have a telephone[8].

Taking this into account, we defined a pair of subgroups within connected households, considering whether they have any kind of telephone service or not. Connected households 1 are those that do not have a telephone and that have access to the Internet only in telecenters. Connected households 2 are those that have any kind of telephone, fixed or mobile, and have access to the Internet only in telecenters. The criteria for the selection of the groups are shown in Table 3.

Table 3: **Household classification criteria according to their digital poverty level**

	Owns radio	Owns television	Owns telephone	Uses Internet in telecenters	Computer and telecenters household
Extremely Digitally Poor			✗	✗	✗
Digitally Poor				✗	✗
Connected					✗
Connected Households 1			✗	✓	✗
Connected Households 2			✓	✓	✗
Digitally Wealthy					✓

The analysis of Table 4, which shows the results of the grouping, presents relevant information. The first fact that attracts attention is the impact of extremely digitally

---

[7] The document that describes in detail the way such application was made, and further analyzes the description of households according to each group is available from the author upon request.

[8] It should be noted that ENAHO does not gather data on household access to public telephones.

poor people, since over 68% of households are basically receptors of information, in terms of new technologies. The second observation is the reduced number of households with Internet connection, which is less than 1% of the sample. Thirdly, it is important to notice that only one out of four households has Internet access through any means. In fourth place, even if there is a strong connection between economic and digital poverty, there is no exact correspondence. Among the extremely digitally poor households, 40% are not economically poor households; and among those who do not have Internet access through any means (digitally poor people) there is a predominance of non economically poor households (83%). Finally, the characteristics of "connected households 1" attract attention, as the proportion of economically poor households with no telephone but with Internet access is greater (33.45%) than among the digitally poor households (16.07%). Later on, we will return to these observations.

Table 4: **Digital and Economic Poverty Level in Peruvian Households**

| Digital Poverty | Nº of Obs. | (%) | Economic Poverty | | |
			Extremely Poor Household	Not Extremely Poor Household	Not Poor Household	
Extremely Digitally Poor Households	12 198	68.99	26.37	32.64	40.98	100
			96.66	79.26	53.59	
Digitally Poor Households	1 375	7.78	0.58	15.49	83.93	100
			0.24	4.24	12.37	
Connected Households	4 020	22.74	2.56	20.62	76.82	100
			3.09	16.5	33.1	
Connected Households 1	2 281	12.9	4.47	28.98	66.55	100
			3.06	13.16	16.27	
Connected Households 2	1 739	9.84	0.06	9.66	90.28	100
			0.03	3.34	16.83	
Digitally Wealthy Households	87	0.49	0	0	100	100
			0	0	0.93	
Total	17 680	100	3 328	5 024	9 328	
			18.82	28.42	52.76	100
			100	100	100	

Source: ENAHO 2003

It is important to take a closer look at the characteristics of the different groups. Firstly, we will observe the demographic characteristics of the households and their members. Afterwards, we will examine the characteristics related to infrastructure and geography, and finally, the economic characteristics.

5.1. DEMOGRAPHIC CHARACTERISTICS

Figure 2 shows the household constitution per age group. It is important to note that among connected people, youths between the ages of 13 and 28 are above the national average and above the average for digitally wealthy people.

Figure 2: **Average number of household members by age group**

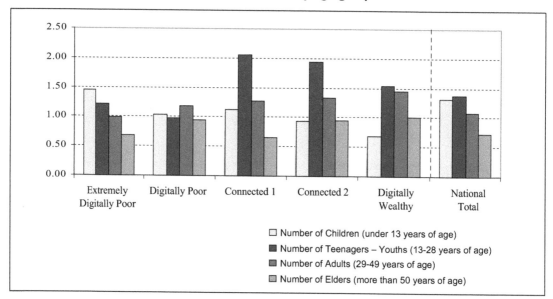

Source: ENAHO 2003

Figure 3: **Illiteracy in households**

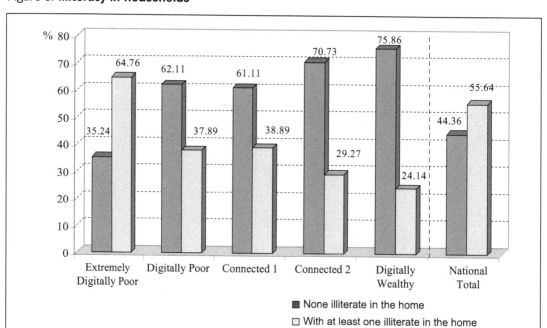

Source: ENAHO 2003

The presence of illiterate individuals in the household constitutes a factor that creates an important difference between groups. Firstly, notice that more than half of the Peruvian households have at least one illiterate member. Among the groups, the gradient is clearly negative: the less connected the household, the higher the proportion of households with at least one illiterate member, as can be seen in Figure 3.

In contrast to the data related to illiteracy, Figure 4 shows the maximum educational level reached by any of the household members. The most interesting fact is that there is practically no difference between digitally poor households and connected households 1, where the maximum educational level attained by any member is complete high school. Households that have completed superior education predominate in connected households 2 and among digitally wealthy people.

Figure 4: **Maximum educational level attained by any household member**

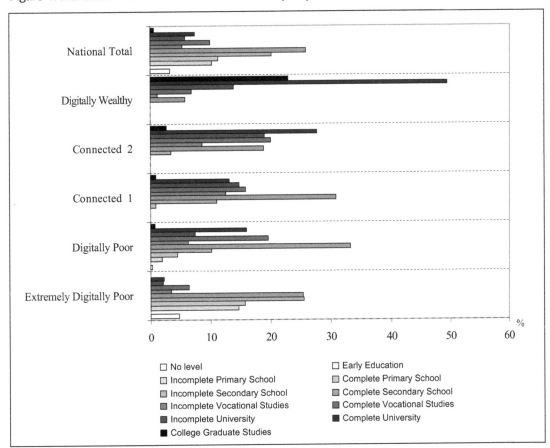

Source: ENAHO 2003

The educational level attained by the head of the household also differs between the groups, as shown in Figure 5. Even though the majority of members of Poor and Connected Households have completed their high school education, among Connected Households 1 many heads of the household have only attended primary school or have completed some grades.

Figure 5: **Educational Level Attained by the Head of the Household**

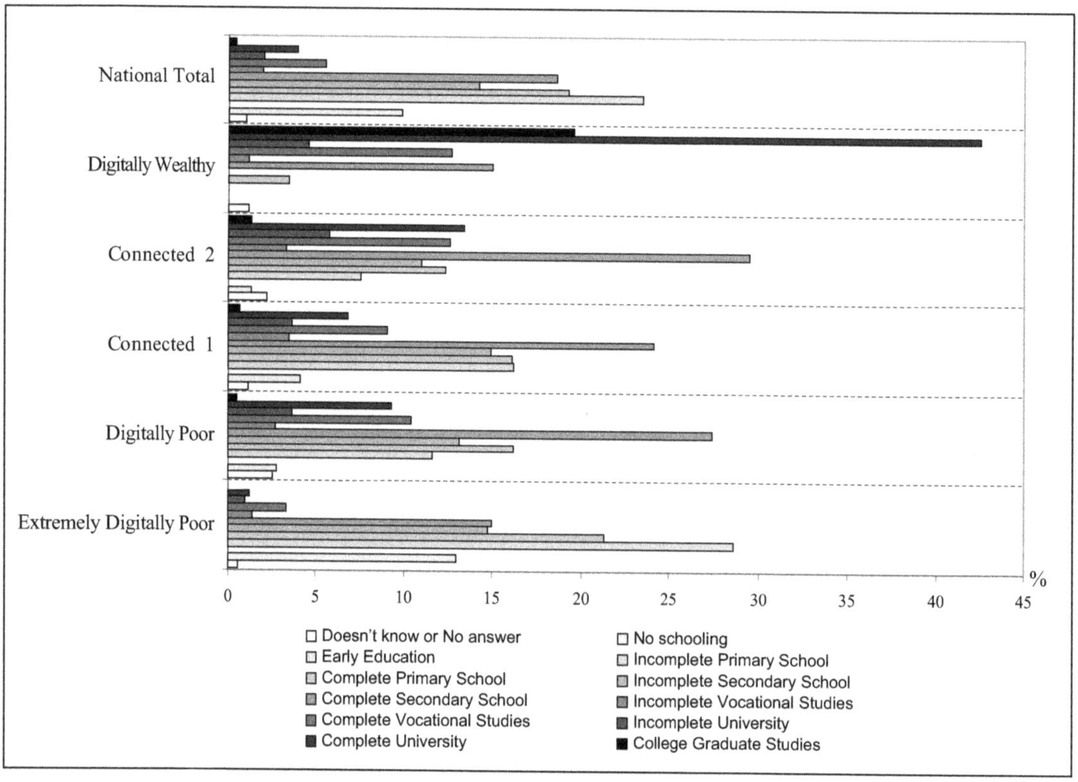

Source: ENAHO 2003

5.2. INFRASTRUCTURE AND GEOGRAPHY

This analysis shows the relevance of supply conditions in the digital poverty level.

The level of access to public services in general is quite limited among the extremely digitally poor people. The connected people are worse in average than the digitally poor people, while the digitally wealthy people have total access to all other public services. Figure 6 includes these comparisons.

Figure 6: **Household access to Public Services**

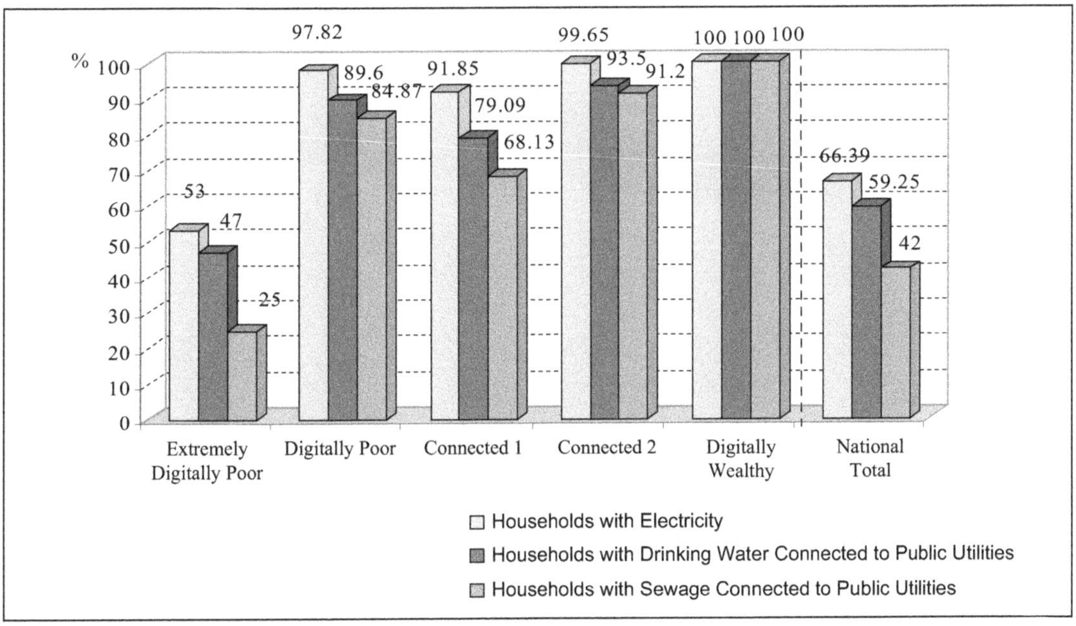

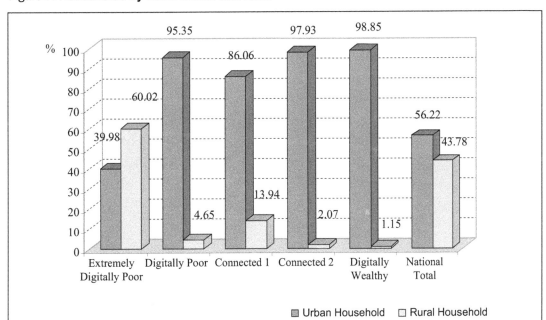

Source: ENAHO 2003

Regarding the urban–rural composition shown in Figure 7, we highlight two characteristics. On the one hand, urban households predominate within digitally poor people. On the other hand, in Connected Households 1, more than 10% belong to rural areas.

Figure 7: **Households by zone: urban and rural**

Source: ENAHO 2003

Geographical regions are strongly marked in Peru (Figure 8): the Coast, the region with the highest relative development, the Mountains, and the Rainforest, the largest region with the greatest communication difficulties. Extremely digitally poor people live mostly in the Mountains, while digitally poor people are concentrated on the Coast. More than half of the Connected People 1 live on the Coast, but over a third live in the Mountains. Connected People 2 and digitally wealthy people again show the expected gradient, with a high predominance of households being located on the Coast.

Figure 8: **Households by geographical location**

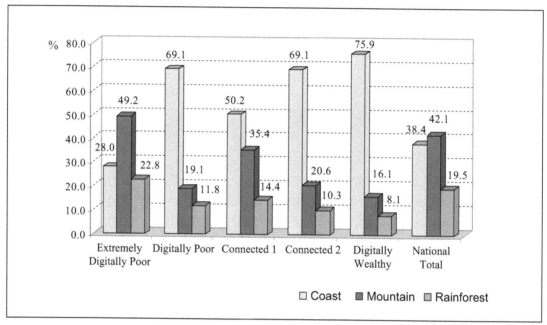

Source: ENAHO 2003

5.3. ECONOMIC CHARACTERISTICS

Concerning the main activity of the head of the household (Figure 9), extremely digitally poor people undertake agricultural or farming activities, while wealthy people undertake service activities. It is important to note that unemployed people prevail among the digitally poor individuals, while heads of the households who undertake service activities prevail among the connected people. Among Connected People 2, there is a large number of households where the head of the household is unemployed.

Figure 10 shows the average income level per group, and the portion of expenses committed to transportation and communications. The outcomes for extremely poor people and for wealthy people are obvious: higher income levels are associated with greater amounts committed to transportation and communication expenses.

Figure 9: **Main Economic Activity of the Head of the Household**

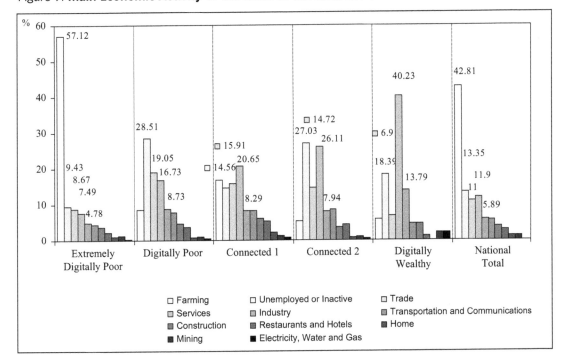

Source: ENAHO 2003

The similarity between poor people and Connected People 2 is important, as they show higher income levels and expense portions than the national total.

5.4. ECONOMETRIC ANALYSIS

The analysis of the data described above shows that differences between extremely poor people and wealthy people are very clear and can be attributed to factors that explain economic poverty: educational level, income, main economic activity, urban condition, etc. What is interesting about the data on Peruvian households is the difference between poor and connected people, who are very similar except for Internet access. For that reason, we try to explain the probability of a household belonging to any of those groups, according to the set of variables analyzed that belong to the conceptual framework.

The listing of the variables considered in explaining this fact, the way of measuring them, and the expected sign are shown in Table 5. The economic poverty level is approximated by variables based on the households' monthly income and the number of members of the household who earn an income, as well as whether or not the head of the household undertakes service-related activities. We expect that the lower the poverty level, the higher the likelihood of the household having Internet access.

Figure 10: **Average Total Monthly Income and Ratio of Transportation and Communication Expenditures to Total Expenditures per Household**

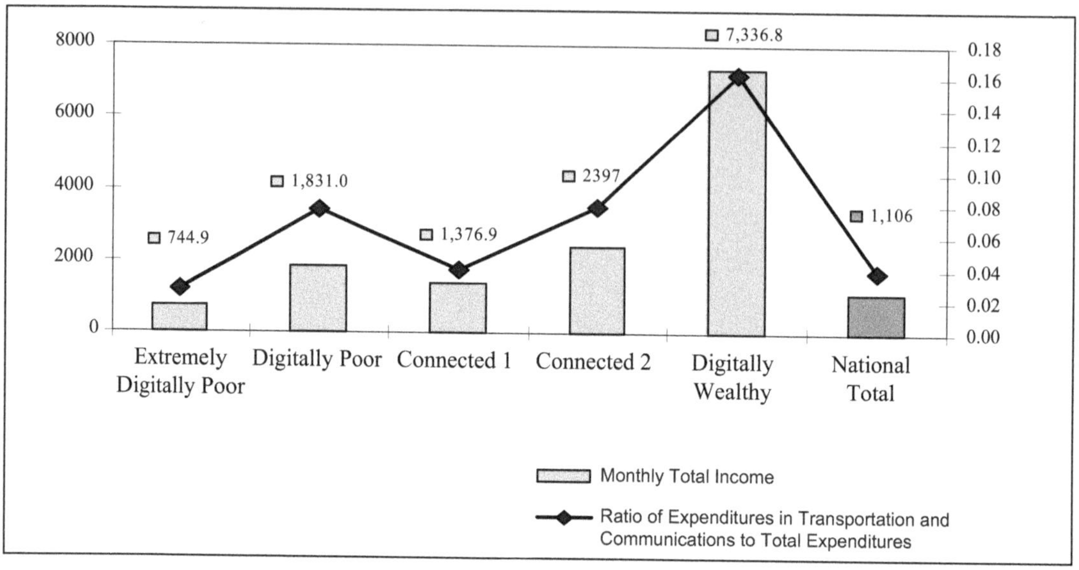

Source: ENAHO 2003

The conceptual framework considers the educational level to be one of the most important variables in explaining an individual's connectivity level. In addition, this is one of the components of the individual's human capital. In this exercise, we approach the human capital of the household by including variables that indicate its different dimensions. As indicated, the estimation of human capital will take into account the size of the family, the educational quality and level attained by the most educated member, and the presence of illiterate individuals. Within the conceptual framework, age is also important to explain the digital poverty level. This is why we used two variables: the ratio of the number of youths in the household (members between 13 and 28 years of age) and the age of the head of the household. Finally, we also included the predominant gender through the male ratio. Human capital variables have a positive influence on the probability of having Internet access, except for the age of the head of the household.

Internet supply is indicated in two ways. On the one hand we separated rural from urban households; the hypothesis is that urban households have a vaster supply of telecommunication services than rural households. On the other hand, we classified the household location: Coast, Mountains or Rainforest, where the Coast is the region with the highest supply of public utilities in general. We do not have a reliable variable to indicate whether the household has Internet access[9].

---

[9] An exercise was carried out to identify whether or not the household district had a telecenter by assigning such requirement to the capitals of districts, provinces, and departments. As the condition was assigned but not verified, and the results were very poor, it was decided not to include it in the final model.

Finally, we introduced three control variables in order to consider the effect of the lack of a telephone in households with Internet access in telecenters. The data collected shows that Connected People 1 are poorer than Connected People 2, and than the digitally poor. In addition, there are other differences regarding demographic characteristics, such as the number of youths and the age of the head of the household. These differences had a negative influence over the model specification, so it was necessary to control them[10].

Table 5: **Summary of Variables, Indicators and Expected Sign**

Theoretical variable	Variable	Indicator	Expected sign
Explained variable			
Connected household	Probability of a household being "connected"	0 = Digitally poor household 1 = Connected household	
Explanatory variables			
Economic Poverty	Income level	Household's monthly total net income	+
Human Capital	Economic Activity	Services as main economic activity of the head of the household	+
	Number of Income Earners	Number of income earners in the household	+
	Stock Size	Number of household members	+
	Age	Age of the head of the household	−
		Ratio of number of teenagers and youths (13-28) to total number of individuals living in household	+
	Gender	Ratio of number of males to total number of individuals living in household	+
	Quality	Illiterate individuals in household: 0 = Household with no illiterate members 1 = Household with at least one illiterate member	−
		Maximum educational level attained by any household member	+
Supply	Zone	0 = Rural 1 = Urban	+
	Region	1 = Forest 2 = Mountain 3 = Coast	+
Control Variables	Income level of household with mobile telephones		−
	Income level of household with a fixed telephone		−
	Zone (Urban or Rural) given that household is on the Coast and has any kind of telephone		−

[10] Instead of two groups clearly defined – poor and connected people, both with telephones – there was a third group that had not been taken into account: they were the individuals who have access to Internet in telecenters, but do not have telephones.

Table 6: Correlation Matrix

	Total monthly net income	Services as head of household's main economic activity	Number of income earners in household	Number of household members	Age of head of the household	Ratio of number of teenagers and youths to total number of individuals living in household	Ratio of male to total number of individuals living in household	Illiterate members in household	Maximum educational level attained by any household member	Zone	Region	Income level of household with a mobile telephone	Income level of household with a fixed telephone	Zone if there is any kind of telephone in the Coast region
Total monthly net income	1													
Services as head of household's main economic activity	0.1827	1												
Number of income earners in household	0.3385	0.0434	1											
Number of household members	0.1557	-0.0184	0.5068	1										
Age of head of the household	0.0596	-0.1264	0.1738	-0.0653	1									
Ratio of number of teenagers and youths to total number of individuals living in household	0.0591	0.0176	0.2084	0.1525	-0.2676	1								
Ratio of male to total number of individuals living in household	-0.0188	0.0007	-0.0194	-0.0589	-0.0599	0.1201	1							
Illiterate members in household	-0.1724	-0.1285	-0.0057	0.2739	0.024	-0.1581	-0.1014	1						
Maximum educational level attained by any household member	0.4833	0.3382	0.3289	0.1842	-0.0921	0.1976	-0.0007	-0.3247	1					
Zone	0.3289	0.2099	0.2176	-0.0057	-0.0139	0.0918	-0.0426	-0.2954	0.4737	1				
Region	0.2039	0.0364	0.1524	-0.0331	0.0713	-0.0078	-0.0323	-0.1385	0.1804	0.3029	1			
Income level of household with a mobile telephone	0.7238	0.1126	0.1208	0.0226	0.0198	0.0116	-0.0185	-0.086	0.2495	0.1482	0.13	1		
Income level of household with a fixed telephone	0.8105	0.1334	0.2233	0.0642	0.0954	0.015	-0.0466	-0.1538	0.3891	0.258	0.1657	0.6496	1	
Zone if there is any kind of telephone in the Coast region	0.394	0.1089	0.1907	0.0345	0.088	0.0179	-0.0464	-0.1847	0.3365	0.3365	0.4332	0.3315	0.5008	1

Table 6 shows the correlation matrix between variables. The relationships between variables are quite weak, except for a high correlation between the control variables and the income; however, this does not affect the assumption of the model's lack of multicolinearity[11].

The econometric results of the Probit model, which explains the probability of a household being connected, reflect what was expected, and are exhibited in Table 7[12]. The most interesting information appears in the last column, which shows the marginal effects, that is, how much the probability of being connected increases, if the value of the explanatory variable increases by 1%. The greatest marginal effect is caused by the relative importance of youths living in the family, immediately followed by one of the supply indicators, the geographical region. The existence of illiterate members in the household reduces the probability of being connected, as does the importance of the males in the family. The sign of the control variables is negative, which indicates that, if the household has a telephone, the probability of having Internet access in telecenters is lower as the income increases. In other words, it seems that the supply characteristics in Peru show that connectivity for economically poor people is obtained through Internet access in telecenters as a substitute for telephones.

6. Conclusions and Perspectives

The concepts of poverty and ICT have been discussed in this chapter to offer a definition of digital poverty that would in turn enable measurement of the level of digital poverty. Our final objective is to design effective policies to reduce digital poverty, as we have defined it. The role played by ICT in the development and reduction of economic poverty has been taken into account.

Our discussion began with basic notions regarding consumer demand, focusing our analysis on income availability and the knowledge of the product/service to calculate its demand. Therefore, it is essential to understand ICT as multidimensional products and services with three basic attributes: connectivity, communication and information. Each one of these attributes may, at the same time, be analyzed through different variables, which will be useful when trying to measure digital poverty.

Digital poverty is therefore defined as a lack of ICT with regards to access and use of the information and communications allowed by the technology. Digital poverty, as here defined, might be a feature of every population segment, whether or not

---

[11] It was proved through partial regressions among explanatory variables.

[12] A simple explanation of the model can be found in Kennedy (1994).

Table 7: Probability of a Household Being "Connected" and Not "Digitally Poor"
(0 = Digitally Poor Household and Connected Household 1)

Variables	Coefficient	Marginal Effect dF/dx
Household's monthly total net income	0.0002166 (0.0000284)	0.0000568
Services as main economic activity of the head of the household	0.2002463 (0.0566007)	0.0497319
Number of income earners in the household	0.1040731 (0.023945)	0.0272861
Number of household members	0.1162496 (0.0137486)	0.0304786
Age of the head of the household	-0.0043565 (0.0016341)	-0.0011422
Ratio of teenagers and youths to total number of individuals living in household	1.412318 (0.0932168)	0.3702852
Ratio of males to total number of individuals living in household	-0.3174351 (0.0904497)	-0.0832259
Illiterate members in household	-0.2428592 (0.0488157)	-0.0656798
Maximum educational level attained by any household member	0.1463263 (0.0131151)	0.0383642
Zone	0.2003845 (0.0890014)	0.0565429
Region	0.5498609 (0.0448043)	0.1441639
Household income level with a mobile telephone	-0.0001654 (0.0000217)	-0.0000434
Household income level, with a fixed telephone	-0.000204 (0.0000233)	-0.0000535
Urban zone in the Coast region with any kind of telephone	-1.309092 (0.0713144)	-0.378221
Constant	-2.245768 (0.195478)	
Number of Observations	5,395	
Pseudo R2	0.2678	
Rate of Model's Predictability	80.59%	
Goodness-Of-Fit Tests	0.806	

Standard errors are indicated in parenthesis.

economically poor. Three types of causes for digital poverty are determined: lack of supply, that is, lack of connectivity access (one of ICT's attributes); lack of demand, a problem clearly related to inadequate income; and lack of need or capacity, which is the problem of non-poor people with no access or use due to age or inadequate literacy. Each kind of digital poverty will require a different public policy.

The approach used for measuring digital poverty has more similarities with the one used for estimating unfulfilled basic needs than with the one used to find the deficit when purchasing a basic family food basket. To that extent, those individuals who neither have access to ICT nor use the digital means enabling information and communication will be considered digitally poor people. In turn, those who do have access and use such means will be connected at different levels.

The approach presented in the conceptual framework requires identifying the uses assigned to ICT to determine not only the connectivity component – which is the most studied one –, but also the component that indicates the types of usage related to connectivity. In other words, if ICT demand is understood as the demand for the attributes of connectivity (information consumption, making information available, or communication), the empirical exercise we carried out with the Peruvian ENAHO explored only one of the ICT demand attributes – the connectivity attribute.

In this application, the term "digital" has been summarized as Internet access, considering it the digital means of information transmission and communication par excellence. The access to and the use of digital mobile telephone services has remained unanalyzed due to data limitations, as well as digital television due to limitations in supply.

Based on Peruvian data, it is important to note that two-thirds of the households qualify as extremely digitally poor households, in contrast to 18% of the households considered extremely economically poor households. It is also interesting to note that extreme digital poverty is an important phenomenon among non economically poor people, which demands developing new ways to actively integrate these groups.

One of the most interesting results of this research study is the importance of households with no telephones, but with access to the Internet in telecenters. There is a comment to add in this regard to the gradient shown in the conceptual framework. One possible explanation is Peru's low telephone service penetration, which seems to make telecenters that offer Internet access a natural substitute for providing communication and entertainment to the public, particularly the youngest members of the household. This is especially relevant to economically poor people, who resort to telecenters as a means of overcoming their lack of communication. Replacing telephones for telecenters to access the Internet is valid when there is a majority of young members living in the household and a relatively young head of the household. The effect is reduced if there are illiterate individuals living in the household.

A variety of research areas for further study have sprung from this exploratory exercise. On the one hand, using household data may allow for a more detailed study of each group's characteristics, particularly of the extremely digitally poor group of individuals, to identify policies focused on the specific restrictions that would need to be overcome to effectively reduce digital poverty. On the other hand, the ad hoc application of the conceptual framework, by carrying out a survey to determine different "digital" uses among individuals through Internet or mobile telephone services may be in place. An in-depth study of the purpose, time, applications, individual learning mechanisms, and the demand for information and communications reflected by the different uses would be a step towards designing policies to overcome digital poverty.

References

ALADI. (2003). *La Brecha Digital y sus Repercusiones en los Países Miembros de la ALADI [The Digital Divide and Its Impact on ALADI Member Countries]*, Asociación Latinoamericana de Integración [Latin American Association for Integration] – ALADI, 194 pp. Retrieved from http://www.aladi.org/nsfaladi/titulare.nsf/5c424a97a14f01e0032568e00046db1b/fa8db613acb8 beee03256d74004dcd3a/$FILE/157Rev1.doc.

ENAHO (Encuesta Nacional de Hogares). (2004). Lima, Peru: Instituto Nacional de Estadística e Informática.

ETS. (2002). *Digital Transformation. A Framework for ICT Literacy. A report of the International ICT literacy panel.* Retrieved May 16, 2005, from http://www.ets.org/research/ictliteracy/ictreport.pdf

INEI. (2003). Encuesta Nacional De Hogares sobre Condiciones de Vida y Pobreza [National Household Survey on Living Standards and Poverty] - ENAHO 2003, Instituto Nacional de Estadística e Informática [National Institute of Statistics and Computer Science] - INEI, Data Base.

ITU. (2003). *New Digital Access Index.* International Telecommunications Union, ITU. p. 6-17. Retrieved May 29, 2005, from http://www.itu.int/ITU-D/ict/dai/material/DAI_ITUNews_s.pdf.

Kennedy, P. (1994). *A Guide to Econometrics.* Third Edition. Cambridge, M.A.: MIT Press.

NTIA. (1999). Falling Through the Net: *Defining the Digital Divide, A Report on the Telecommunications and Information Technology Gap in America.* National Telecommunications and Information Administration (NTIA). Retrieved May 7th, 2005, from http://www.ntia.doc.gov/ntiahome/fttn99/FTTN.pdf

Nyaki, C. (2002). *ICT and Poverty: A Literature Review,* International Development Research Center-IDCR, 58 pp. Retrieved May 27, 2005, from http://network.idrc.ca/uploads/user-S/10541291550ICTPovertyBiblio.doc. http://network.idrc.ca/ev.php?URL_ID=24718&URL_DO=DO_TOPIC&URL_SECTION

ORBICOM. (2003). *Monitoring the Digital Divide…and Beyond.* Orbicom, Canadian Agency for International Development, InfoDev and UNESCO, 161 pp. Retrieved May 10, 2005, from http://www.infodev.org/files/836_file_The_Digital_Divide.pdf.

Varian, H. (2002). *Intermediate Microeconomics.* Spanish Edition. Barcelona: Antoni Bosch.

World Bank. (2002). *Information and Communication Technologies: A World Bank Group Strategy.* Retrieved May 3, 2005, from http://info.worldbank.org/ict/assets/docs/sp_ExecSum.pdf

World Bank. (2003). *ICT and MDGs: A World Bank Group perspective, World Bank Group's Global ICT Department.* Washington D.C. 39 pp. Retrieved April 30, 2005, from http://info.worldbank.org/ict/assets/docs/mdg_Complete.pdf

CHAPTER 3

New Market Scenarios in Latin America

Judith Mariscal, Carla Bonina and Julio Luna

Abstract

This chapter analyzes the role of the market in network expansion in Latin America. Although universal access policies have achieved some degree of success in fighting the digital divide, the issue of massive access to ICT services seems to be more directly associated with the sector's regulatory environment and with the level of competition prevailing in the sector. This chapter describes the expansion process of the major operators in Latin America – Telefónica Spain and Teléfonos Mexico – as a result of regulatory policies implemented in their countries of origin. It evaluates the sector's performance after the reforms carried out in the region, as well as the role of mobile telephone services as the driving force in offering access to population segments that had no previous service. And, lastly, within this new market and technological context, it is suggested that there is a need to design policies that turn challenges into new opportunities to encourage network expansion towards areas without services. Thus, within this new scenario, research lines are identified to carry out regulatory policies and contribute to the enrichment of their design.

This chapter analyzes the role played by the market, as well as by competition and its regulation in network expansion in Latin America. Although universal access programs implemented in the region have achieved varying degrees of success in fighting the digital divide (García-Murillo & Kuerbis, 2004), the issue of massive access to information and communication technologies (ICT) seems to be closely related to the sector's regulation, the market's development and the level of competition prevailing in the sector.

Developing countries have faced the challenge of expanding access to the telecommunications network through two kinds of policies. The first type of policy aims to create a competitive market that stimulates investment, lowers fees and encourages ICT access. The second kind of policy emphasizes a direct role of the public sector in providing access to the population through subsidized programs.

These two kinds of policies reflect the need to fight two phenomena, which the World Bank has called the Market Gap and the Access Gap. The Market Gap refers to the difference between the penetration level that could be reached under non-optimal market conditions and under optimal conditions. The Access Gap refers to the unavoidable market failures where some population groups are not serviced because their access is not considered profitable.

This chapter analyzes the role played by the market in the network expansion in Latin America. More than a decade has gone by since Latin American governments put a pro-market reform within the telecommunications sector into action. In general terms, these reforms have contributed to encouraging the adoption of technology, to expanding service access and to lowering its costs. However, the regulatory models adopted in the region have not yet been able to fully achieve the objectives set forth during this process. In particular, the lack of ICT access is still a significant problem for the lower income population segments. Moreover, although the more general objectives related to the development of the sector remain unchanged, technological innovation and the market context have significantly changed the industry scenario. These changes exert a growing pressure on the traditional models and pose new challenges.

With regard to the market, today, the region experiences a consolidation of two major actors that compete against each other in practically all Latin American countries. While the Spanish company Telefónica consolidated a strong position in many countries within the region starting in the mid-90s, the Mexican company Telmex and its subsidiary América Móvil have recently developed a strong acquisition policy within the local and mobile telephone sectors. These measures pose serious concerns regarding the future of competition in the region. The current regulatory models are still trying to adjust to the improved practices of a scheme that believes the sector can work by increasing its level of competition through a large number of operators. Reality makes us face a different situation, not only a market concentration, but the clear presence of a regional duopoly. Although the operators are already implementing corporate strategies in this new context, the regulators do not seem to have adjusted their policies to this scenario.

In addition, technological innovation has brought about an uneven development of the different market segments, where mobile telephone services have adopted a predominant role in the region. Today, among the population with fewer resources, mobile telephone services represent the main form of access to telecommunications services. The technological convergence opens the possibility of offering similar services through different means. The regulation of technologies associated to a service must be re-evaluated.

The first part of this chapter illustrates the expansion process of the two main operators in Latin America as a result of regulatory policies implemented in their countries of origin. The second part of this paper assesses the performance of the sector after the reforms implemented in the region. The third and last section of this chapter analyzes the role of mobile telephone services as the driving force to give access to previously unattended population segments. Lastly, once this new market and technology context is described, this chapter suggests the need to generate policies that turn new challenges into opportunities to encourage network expansion towards unattended areas. In this regard, research lines are identified to contribute to the enrichment of regulatory policy design within this new scenario.

1. The Expansion of Telefónica and América Móvil[1]

Reforms to the telecommunications sector carried out in Spain and Mexico during the 90s favored the creation of two major companies, placing them in a predominant position in all segments of this market. The strategy implemented in both cases was the result of policies that aimed at creating National Champions. The success of these policies made the globalization of these companies possible.

In the case of Spain, with the imminent access of the European Community Market, the Spanish government implemented policies supporting Telefónica in order for it to face competition. However, Spanish telecommunications needed to be updated the most compared to other European countries, making it highly probable that the company would be acquired by major European operators or, in the best possible scenario, that it would play a subordinate role within integrated European telecommunication services. In order to anticipate this possibility, the Spanish government chose to transform Telefónica into a National Champion.

---

[1] This section is based on Mariscal & Rivera (2005).

The goal of creating a National Champion was re-established as a specific telecommunication policy objective in the document *"Líneas estratégicas de las políticas de telecomunicaciones para el período de transición"* (Strategic Trends in Telecommunication Policies for the Transitional Period). This document asserts the need "to reinforce national operators for them to face competitors from other countries" and proposes to favor the technological and industrial development of the national telecommunications sector.

The regulatory framework established a generous price policy along with a credit policy of "cheap money" and the decision of not distributing dividends. During the first half of the 90s, the price policy aimed at financing the company's modernization and re-balancing its fees. Telefónica benefited from the Spanish government's support through strong financing mechanisms.[2] Telefónica began to acquire

Table 1: **Telefónica's World Positioning By Services**

Grupo Telefónica - Per service in 2003						
Country	Local Telephone Services	Long-Distance Telephone Services	Mobile Telephone Services	Internet	Data	Public Telephone Services
Spain	✓	✓	✓	✓	✓	✓
Argentina	✓	✓	✓	✓	✓	✓
Brazil	✓	✓		✓	✓	
Chile			✓	✓	✓	
Mexico	✓	✓	✓	✓	✓	
Peru	✓	✓	✓	✓	✓	✓

Source: Own study based on data from Telefónica's Web site and information submitted by the company.

Market Participation in Selected Countries		
Country	Fixed Lines	Mobile Users
Spain	52.3%	52.8%
Argentina	55.8%	24.4%
Brazil	33.7%	20.9%
Chile	73.5%	29.8%
Mexico	-	9.2%
Peru	99.6%	55.1%

Source: Own study based on data from Telefónica's Web site. It includes the recent acquisition of mobile operations by Bellsouth in Latin America announced in March 2004. The table does not include less significant company operations in Latin America.

---

[2] This policy was not exclusive of the telecommunications sector, and was also developed in other sectors, such as the infrastructure and banking sectors.

companies with market power and exclusivity periods in Argentina, Chile, Peru and Brazil (Table 1). In these countries, the reforms were made in a context of fiscal crisis, which led to prioritizing fiscal revenues over the creation of a competitive environment, which in turn resulted in an advantage to the buyers. The acquisition process opened an exclusive market in Latin America for the company, which in terms of number of consumers was much larger than the Spanish market. These new markets had an important growth potential, since telephone density was extremely low and the proximity between the three new Latin American markets helped in order to take advantage of economies of scope and of scale.

In the case of Mexico, in 1990 (and as a vital part of the country's modernization program), Telmex was privatized and sold as a vertically integrated company. Achieving a successful privatization meant to overcome all political and economic hurdles faced by policy-makers. A vertically integrated company served the objective of meeting the demands of the key players in the system: the national private sector and the unions, who lobbied against dismantling the company and favored the creation of a National Champion. In addition, policy-makers considered that dividing Telmex would take longer, during a period when time was a key factor to determine the success of the modernization program. Telmex was financially strengthened, making it more attractive to investors, and was sold in 1990 to the joint venture between the Mexican consortium Grupo Carso, Southwestern Bell and France Telecom. Later on, Grupo Carso began to acquire shares, becoming the major shareholder in Telmex-América Móvil.

The Mexican group Telmex-América Móvil did not play a significant role at the beginning of the privatization process in Latin America. Operations focused their attention on the Mexican company's modernization efforts. The country's great growth potential, given a penetration of little over 6% in fixed telephone services, made this option viable. The priority was to strengthen the company and to prepare it for future competition as a result of the eventual entry of powerful U.S. operators into the country.

Its interest in the Latin American telecommunications sector began during the second half of the 90s, and followed two different paths: i) acquisitions of privatized fixed telephone companies in Guatemala, El Salvador and Nicaragua, and, most importantly, ii) the expansion of their mobile telephone operations in several countries in South America (Table 2).

Table 2: **Telmex América Móvil World Positioning Per Services**

Telmex-América Móvil 2003-2004

Telmex (1) – América Móvil (2) Positioning

Country	Service					
	Local Telephone Services	Long-Distance Telephone Services	Mobile Telephone Services	Internet	Data	Public Telephone Services
Argentina (1, 2)		✓	✓	✓	✓	
Brazil (1, 2)	✓	✓	✓	✓	✓	
Chile (1)	✓	✓		✓	✓	
Colombia (1, 2)			✓	✓	✓	
Ecuador (2)			✓			
El Salvador, Honduras and Nicaragua (2)	✓	✓	✓		✓	
Guatemala (2)	✓	✓	✓	✓	✓	
Mexico (1, 2)	✓	✓	✓	✓	✓	✓
Peru (1)	✓	✓		✓	✓	

Note: (1) Indicates Telmex's presence, (2) América Móvil's presence and (1, 2) both companies' presence in each case.

América Móvil's Market Share in Latin America At the end of 2004	
Country	**Mobile Market Share (% of Users)**
Argentina	27.8
Brazil	25.6
Chile	- -
Colombia	57.5
Ecuador	63.9
El Salvador	32.2
Guatemala	45.6
Honduras	28.3
Mexico	75.6
Nicaragua	58.1
Panama	- -
Peru	- -
Uruguay	1.0
Venezuela	- -

Source: Own study based on América Móvil's 2004 Annual Report.

In contrast to Telefónica, which built its competitive position in Latin America by acquiring local fixed telephone services in several countries and soon after or even simultaneously entering other segments, Telmex and América Móvil first entered those markets with mobile and long-distance telephone services. In many countries the rate of mobile telephone penetration has exceeded the rate of fixed telephone services, reducing the need to control the fixed telephone services local loop. Perhaps it is even more important that mobile telephone services are beginning to offer broadband Internet access, with a quality that can compete with DSL or Cable TV technology. Moreover, Telmex-América Móvil's strategy for the region was not limited to mobile or long-distance telephone services – it also had a global strategy that included local fixed telephone services.

Telefónica has followed an aggressive expansion policy in recent years. The most important acquisition has been the franchise of local fixed telephone services in Brazil, which has led to control of one-third of the telephone lines in Latin America's biggest country. At the same time, it has acquired all of Bellsouth's mobile telephone operations in Latin America. With this acquisition, Telefónica reached 55 million mobile telephone users in the region at the end of 2004 (Table 3). Moreover, Telefónica has entered the Mexican mobile market and controls 14.8% of total users in that country (Table 4).

Table 3: **Telefónica's Worldwide Results for 2004**

Grupo Telefónica 2004 Revenues and Users				
Country	Spain	Other Countries	Total	% var 04-03
Revenues (1)	24,753.0	16,296.8	41,049.8	6.8
Lines in Service (2)	19,835.3	23,414.3	43,249.5	5.2
Cellular Users (3)	18,977.0	55,465.4	74,442.5	43.6

(1) In millions of Dollars.

(2) Thousands of lines in service: It includes all lines in service from Telefónica Spain, Telefónica CTC Chile, Telefónica Argentina, Telefónica Peru, Telesp, Telefónica Móviles El Salvador, Telefónica Móviles Guatemala and Telefónica Deutschland.

(3) Thousands of mobile users: It includes all cellular users of Telefónica Servicios Móviles Spain, MediTelecom, Telefónica Móvil Chile, TCP Argentina, Telefónica Móviles Peru, Brasilcel (Joint Venture with Portugal Telecom in Brazil), Telefónica Móviles Guatemala, Telefónica Móviles El Salvador, Telefónica Móviles Mexico and the operators acquired from BellSouth in Latin America (Venezuela, Guatemala, Nicaragua, Panama, Ecuador, Colombia, Peru and Uruguay).

Source: Grupo Telefónica 2004 Annual Report

In 2004, América Móvil from Mexico and Telefónica Móviles from Spain operated in 15 Latin American countries, with a joint share in some countries of over 90% such as in the case of Nicaragua, Colombia, Ecuador and Mexico (Table 4). This indicates the presence of a regional duopoly.

Table 4: **Country Presence and Market Share of América Móvil vs. Telefónica Móviles, 2004**

Telefónica Móviles vs. América Móvil 2004 Market Share			
Country / Segment	**AMX (%)**	**TEM (%)**	**AMX+TMX (%)**	**Country's Mobile Density**
Argentina	27.8	26.1	53.8	34
Brazil	25.6	49.8	75.5	37
Chile	- -	35.1	35.1	61
Colombia	57.5	32.6	90.1	23
Ecuador	63.9	30.8	94.7	28
El Salvador	32.2	23.9	56.1	23
Guatemala	45.6	26.2	71.8	23
Honduras	28.3	- -	28.3	10
Mexico	75.6	14.8	90.4	36
Nicaragua	58.1	40.4	98.4	13
Panama	- -	73.1	73.1	12
Peru	- -	51.9	52.0	15
Uruguay	1.0	35.6	36.7	16
Venezuela	- -	45.7	45.7	30

Note: AMX: América Móvil, TEM: Telefónica Móviles. Mobile Density represents total mobile density for the country.

Source: Telecom-CIDE based on information from the companies and regulators' Web pages.

Even when Telefónica arrived first in the majority of the countries, the acquisition process of América Móvil and Telmex has modified the configuration of the market in such a way that, although Telefónica continues to have a greater presence in terms of number of countries and users, América Móvil and Telmex continue expanding into new markets. At the end of 2004, Grupo Telefónica reported significantly higher revenues than Telmex – América Móvil's joint operations. However, the growth rates of the Mexican company are larger in the 2003-2004 fiscal year (Tables 3 and 5). In the fixed telephone services segment, Telefónica continues to hold the dominant position in the region, followed by Telmex, which concentrates the majority of its operations in Mexico. Currently, Telefónica leads in the fixed, mobile and broadband markets in Brazil, Argentina, Chile, Peru and Venezuela, while América Móvil and Telmex have a clear dominance in the same segments in Mexico and Central American countries. In 2005, América Móvil and Telmex have acquired new companies in Brazil, Nicaragua, Honduras, Colombia, Venezuela and Chile. This year, the total net increase of users for América Móvil in the region exceeded 7 million users, while Telefónica's total net increase was 4.5 million users. In the case of Mexico, during the same period, Telefónica reported a loss of 200,000 users.

Table 5: **Telmex-América Móvil 2004 Results in Latin America**

América Móvil 2004 Revenues and Users				
	Mexico	**Other Countries**	**Total**	**% var 04-03**
Revenues from Operations (1)	6,352.0	5,733.0	12,085.0	49.1
Lines in Service (2)	- -	1,896.0	1,896.0	17.1
Mobile Customers (3)	28,851.0	32,258.0	61,109.0	39.2
Telmex 2004 Revenues and Users				
	Mexico	**Other Countries**	**Total**	**% var 04-03**
Revenues from Operations (4)	11,034.2	1,409.9	12,444.1	12.9
Lines in Service (5)	17,172.3	No Data	17,172.3	9.5

(1) In millions of Dollars.

(2) Thousands of lines in service. It includes the number of fixed lines in El Salvador, Nicaragua and Guatemala.

(3) Thousands of mobile customers: It includes all customers in Mexico, United States, Guatemala, El Salvador, Honduras, Nicaragua, Colombia, Ecuador, Brazil, Uruguay and Argentina.

Source: América Móvil 2004 Annual Report.

(4) In millions of Dollars.

(5) Thousands of lines in service.

Source: Telmex 2004 Annual Report.

The reform of the telecommunications sector in Latin America has resulted in the unexpected consolidation of two operators that seem to turn the market into a regional duopoly. This poses serious concerns for the development of competition, since a duopoly can generate oligopoly-like practices. Experience has shown that a larger number of operators generate greater competition, and the latter is more efficient in promoting the sector's development by lowering prices, improving quality and expanding the infrastructure (Li & Colin, 2002; Gutiérrez, 2003; Wallsten 2000, 2001).

In their expansion process, both companies have proven to be able to operate strategically and defeat their competitors. In several countries, policies aimed at controlling their expansion and market power have had little success. It would seem reasonable to expect market segmentation strategies and an alliance between both companies; however, this does not seem to be the case until now, since both companies have continued with an expansion process in the same countries and market segments. This phenomenon could be associated to cultural and organizational differences in both companies. While Telmex is vertically operated from Mexico, all of Telefónica's companies report to Spain, and, in some degree, they have underestimated the capacity of the Mexican company to challenge Telefónica's power in Latin America. Today what we can observe is a global survival strategy. In fact, both companies have sacrificed profits in several countries (as shown in the following section) and are taking advantage of the economies of scale and of scope created by their size and regional positioning. As long as the Latin American market is still growing, either from unmet demand or from demand for new services, it is foreseeable that competition and not collusion will prevail.

2. The Sector's Performance

Certainly the impact of the reform on the telecommunications sector has been positive. The sector's performance, measured by traditionally used indicators, shows that this market has made major progress in increasing its levels as well as its growth

Figure 1: **Fixed Teledensity Evolution in Latin America 1990-2003**

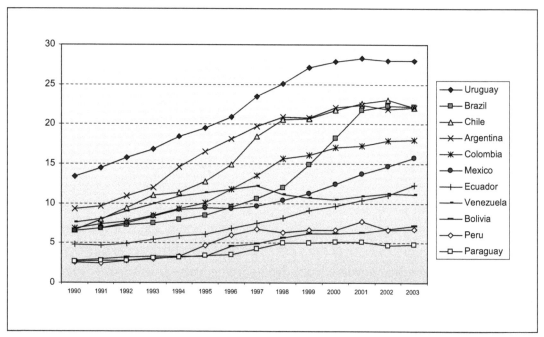

Sources: Telecom Data-CIDE based on ITU World Telecommunication Indicators 2004 and World Development Indicators 2004.

rates. During the 90s, the period when the first series of telecommunication reforms took place, the Latin American economy exhibited a modest positive performance in its economic growth of close to 2% averaged among the 11 main economies in the region, led by Argentina, Chile and Uruguay. Despite this moderate growth, the modernization efforts in the region translated into the privatization and financial liberalization processes that led to a record growth in telephone services, with an average annual growth rate of over 12%. As shown in Figure 1, telephone density doubled in the region on average terms during this period.

Figure 2: **Telephone Lines per Employee – Comparison between Latin America and the European Union**

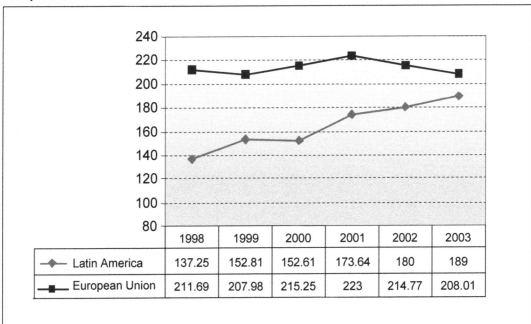

	1998	1999	2000	2001	2002	2003
Latin America	137.25	152.81	152.61	173.64	180	189
European Union	211.69	207.98	215.25	223	214.77	208.01

Sources: Telecom Data-CIDE based on ITU World Telecommunication Indicators 2004 and World Development Indicators 2004.

Along with the increase in teledensity, the improvements made in network modernization and the efficiency in the companies' operations added to the benefits brought about by reforms. In terms of technological adoption, by the end of the decade the percentage of digital lines in the region exceeded 90%. Figure 2 shows the companies' productivity. The number of lines per employee also points towards an accelerated growth path that tends to reach efficiency levels similar to those of European markets. In addition, tariffs have shown a tendency to decrease in most market segments.

However, the objectives of the reform have been unevenly reached among the different countries and within each country's regions. The results of the privatization, with different modalities and timing, were better in Chile (the first country to privatize), Brazil (among the last ones to privatize) and finally Uruguay which, in a nationalistic impulse, refused to privatize but made extraordinary advances in indirect ways, reaching the highest fixed telephone service density of the region by the end of the decade (28%). On the other hand, the region's poorer countries – Bolivia, Peru and Paraguay – kept the lowest penetration levels of the region, below 6%, during the entire period.

Table 6: **Fixed Teledensity from the Perspective of Revenues in Latin American Countries**

Country	pcGDP US$ct95 2003*	Gini Index 2000	Fixed teledensity 2003
Uruguay	4,953	.45	28
Brazil	4,182	.58	22
Chile	6,051	.57	22
Argentina	6,601	.52	22
Colombia	2,352	.58	18
Mexico	4,682	.55	16
Ecuador	1,855	.44	12
Venezuela	2,470	.49	11
Bolivia	939	.45	7.2
Peru	2,431	.50	7
Paraguay	1,235	No Data	5

* GDP per capita in constant US$ (1995).

Source: Telecom Data-CIDE based on ITU World Telecommunication Indicators 2004 and World Development Indicators 2004.

Table 6 shows the inequalities among countries in terms of fixed telephone service expansion for 2003. The inequalities in performance do not seem to correspond to unequal wealth, as could be expected. Brazil, which had a very similar income to Mexico that year, reached a teledensity of 22 lines per 100 inhabitants, while Mexico had 16 lines. In turn, Chile, with a lower GNP per capita, also reached 22 lines per 100 inhabitants.

In addition, within the countries, the achievements in terms of penetration and access are also very uneven. There is an internal growth gap between regions with higher access in contrast to those with lower telephone penetration levels, showing rates well below the national average. It is noticeable that this limitation caused by inequalities within countries is observed across the region. Most of the infrastructure is concentrated in the metropolitan area of the capital city, in contrast to the marginal services offered in rural areas (Figure 3). For example, in the case of Mexico and Argentina, some provinces/regions show low penetration levels, such as the case of Chiapas and Chaco, with six times less teledensity than the capital cities and metropolitan areas. The most dramatic case continues to be Peru, where in 2003 the region of Lima had a penetration level close to 30 times higher than the province of Huancavelica, with a fixed teledensity of 0.48.

Figure 3: **Internal Gap in Telephone Services (% of Teledensity) – Selected Countries in Latin America, 2003**

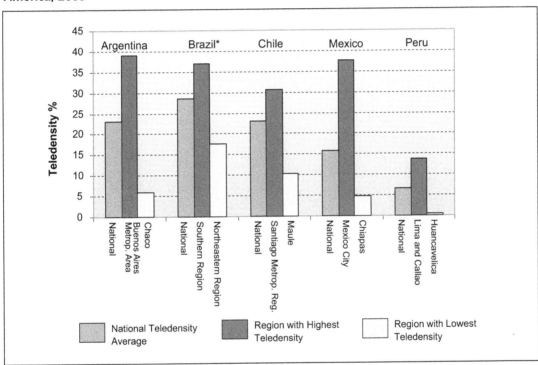

Source: Own study based on data from: CNC (Argentina), Anatel (Brazil), Subtel (Chile), Cofetel (Mexico) and MTC (Peru). Data from end of 2003. *Brazil: data for 2002.

There is ample literature on descriptive and empirical studies that discuss the issue of performance differences based on the reforms implemented. Outcomes are consistent with the conventional consensus and we know that competition continues to be the best mechanism to encourage the sector's development by increasing penetration and lowering fees (Wallsten, 2000). In addition, privatization by itself does not cause the same impact if not combined with the creation of an independent regulator (Li & Colin Xu, 2002). Empirical studies indicate that the most important variables to explain the sector's performance are the level of competition, the sequence in policy implementation and the exclusivity periods granted (Wallsten, 2000).

The region's performance, measured by the growth in fixed density, has slowed down and has been stagnant since 1998 as can be observed in Figure 7. This was caused, among other reasons, by the exclusivity periods, the high costs of installing the network and the lack of profitability of the service in rural areas. During the

Figures 4 and 5: **Market Concentration and Teledensity**

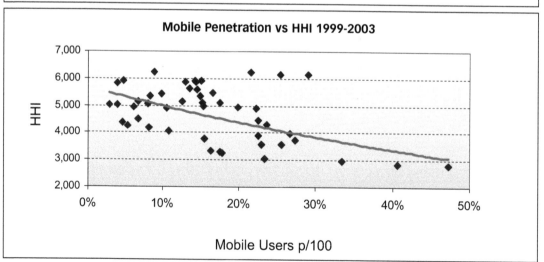

Source: Telecom-CIDE based on companies' information and regulators' Web pages.

same year, mobile telephone services, as an alternative market, together with changes in technology began to experience an accelerated process of growth, creating great expectations in terms of foreign investment and business opportunities, enjoying the advantage of a lesser regulatory dependence and the need for survival of the dominant fixed telephone service companies.

The perspective for the sector's performance, within a regional duopoly in the making, presents the potential difficulties that are usually associated with this phenomenon in terms of price, service quality and network expansion (Shy, 1995). In a merely descriptive analysis, the observed data of concentration, measured by using the Herfindahl-Hirschman Index (HHI)[3] and its relationship to the performance of telephone services as measured using the teledensity recorded in both segments, were studied. The following Figures 4 and 5 show that high HHI levels are associated with relatively lower teledensity levels. The same applies for fixed as well as mobile telephone services.

While the data presented are not conclusive and require a greater methodological rigor, it can be inferred that there is a negative relationship between both indicators, which is shown most significantly in the case of fixed telephone services, that is a market traditionally operated by companies with high concentrations at national or regional level. In the case of the mobile telephone market, this relationship has been developed from a higher level of competition, and currently has a better performance level in comparison to fixed telephone services, as will be documented in the following section of this chapter.

In 2001, the market experienced an important change in almost all countries in the region. The overtaking of fixed telephone services by mobile telephone services was driven mainly by the introduction of the pre-paid system and "Calling Party Pays" (CPP), which was part of the redesign process of the companies' business model. In 2000-2003, the average growth in users of mobile telephony was 33% in the region, while that of traditional telephone services recorded a much lower 7%. In this new scenario, the telecommunications market entered into a consolidation process where mobile telephone services became the main focus of the two major operators in the region: América Móvil and Telefónica Móviles. The acquisition process of these two companies involved an aggressive campaign to attract customers and the depredation of local markets fighting for the regional positioning, even at the expense of lowering the revenues per user. Figure 6 shows a reduction in the Average Revenues Per User (ARPU) during this period, both in the total amount as well as in ARPU per

---

[3] The Herfindahl-Hirschman Index is a measure generally accepted to determine the market concentration level. It is computed based on the sum of the squared market share of each company; the indicator assigns values between 0 and 10,000, where the greater the value, the higher the market concentration.

Figure 6: **Average Revenues Per User in Latin America (ARPU)**

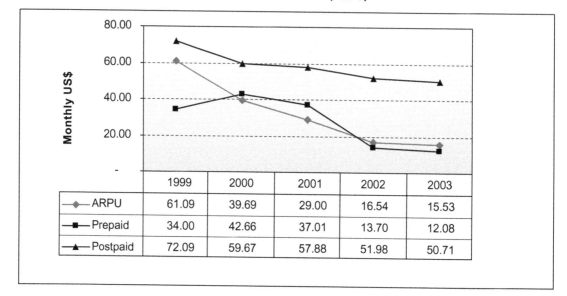

	1999	2000	2001	2002	2003
ARPU	61.09	39.69	29.00	16.54	15.53
Prepaid	34.00	42.66	37.01	13.70	12.08
Postpaid	72.09	59.67	57.88	51.98	50.71

Sources: Telecom Data-CIDE based on ITU World Telecommunication Indicators 2004 and World Development Indicators 2004.

service, together with an increase in the user base. This indicates the presence of a global survival scenario and not an alliance between companies.

3. The Role of Mobile Telephone Services[4]

In recent years, in the region and in the world, mobile telephone services show a level of dynamism and growth that is much greater than that of fixed telephone services. This contributes to significantly increased access to telecommunications services. However, universal access policies continue to focus on promoting fixed line connectivity and Internet access.

The introduction of mobile telephones in the region has contributed significantly to increasing the access to telecommunications services, and thus it has helped to close the digital divide. Figure 7 illustrates the evolution of fixed and mobile telephone services in the region, while Figure 8 shows the evolution in the amount of mobile users per fixed line. With no exceptions, the countries involved in the sample show a tendency to an increase in mobile users per fixed line, particularly Mexico and Chile, where a higher volume of mobile users in contrast to fixed users can be observed since 1999.

---

[4] In strict technological terms, cellular and mobile telephones are different. Mobile telephone services include cellular telephone services (which operate in 800 or 1900 MHz bands) more than any other technology that is not operated in these bands, such as trunking. However, in this chapter both terms are used indistinctively.

Figure 7: **Mobile vs. Fixed Penetration in Selected Countries**

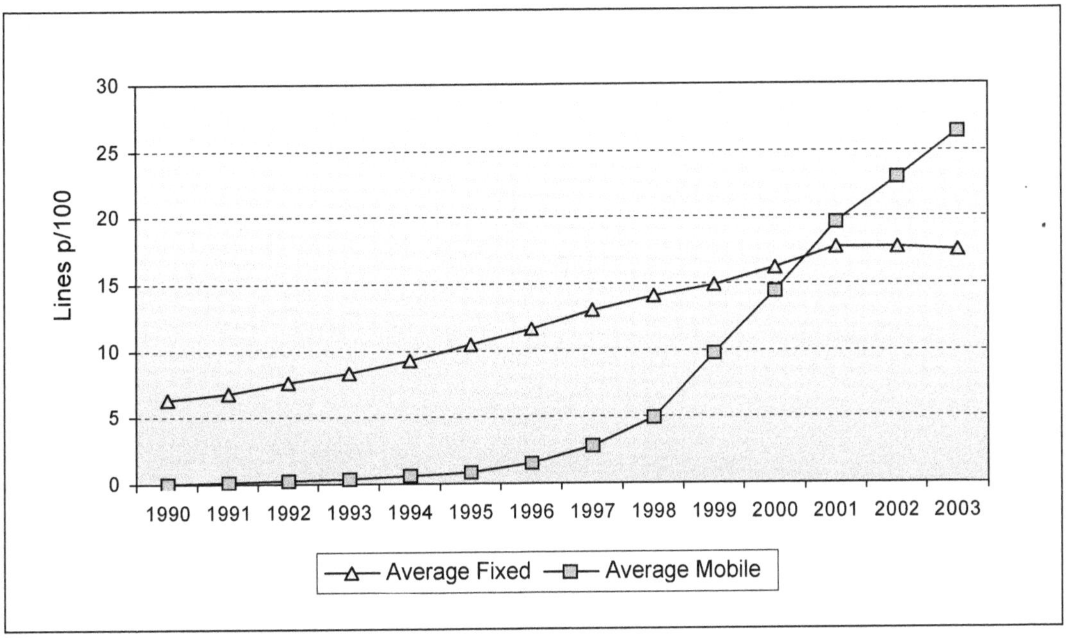

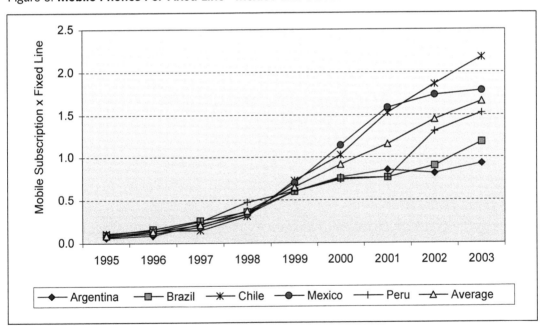

Source: Telecom-DATA based on ITU and data obtained from regulators. Note: Average teledensity corresponds to the five countries involved in the sample (Argentina, Brazil, Chile, Mexico and Peru).

Figure 8: **Mobile Phones Per Fixed Line - Mexico and Selected Countries in Latin America**

Source: Telecom-DATA based on ITU and data obtained from regulators and operators.

A phenomenon that has certainly contributed to the increase in mobile and cellular growth in the region is the new pricing structure: the pre-paid card and "Calling Party Pays" (CCP). Clearly, the pre-paid option in Latin America has become a very powerful tool to encourage universal access, due to its convenience for lower income population segments. As illustrated in Figure 9, four of every five users in the region choose the pre-paid option over any other plan. In the case of Mexico, the difference is even more significant, since over 90% of users prefer this option.

Figure 9: **Pre-Paid Mobile Telephone Services in the Region**

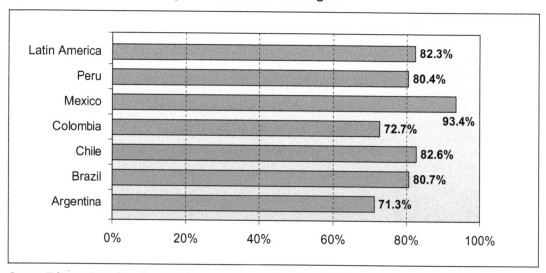

Source: Telecom-DATA based on data from operators and regulators' Web pages.

Several current studies highlight the advantages of mobile telephone services over traditional telecommunications access, which offers fixed telephone services for low consumption users (Dymond & Oestman, 2004; NECG, 2004; Stephens et al., 2005; Oestman, 2003). One of these advantages is the lower activation cost for the user in the case of mobile services (line activation, SIM card, equipment, etc.), as compared to fixed telephone services.

Another advantage consists of the alternatives offered by the pre-paid option, which allows the user to control costs and avoid signing a contract, thus not having to demonstrate a good credit history. For the operator it means not having to send monthly account balances and avoiding the risk of users failing to make contract payments.

The following table compares the initial and the monthly usage costs for users with low fixed and mobile telephone consumption in some countries in Latin America.

Table 7: **Cost Contrast between Fixed and Mobile Telephone Services for Low Consumption Users**

	Initial Cost		Monthly Cost/Calls	
	Fixed Telephone	**Mobile Telephone**	**Fixed Telephone**	**Mobile Telephone**
Argentina	$150	$50.00	$13.65	$7.95
Brazil	$27	$40.00	$7.90	$4.50
Chile	$43	$67.10	$11.40	$8.10
Colombia	$168	$49.25	$3.70	$4.20
Mexico	$119	$46.20	$16.25	$6.90
Peru	$131	$60.40	$13.95	$4.50
Venezuela	$102	$54.00	$11.60	$6.15
Average	**$105.71**	**$52.42**	**$11.21**	**$6.04**

Note: Amounts in US Dollars. Source: Oestman 2003.

Apart from a few exceptions, in all cases mobile telephone services have lower costs, in terms of initial costs as well as usage costs. On average, as shown in Table 7, the cost of mobile telephone services is close to half that of fixed telephone services. Once more, it is important to highlight that these conclusions are only valid for low consumption users, as previously stated.

In a study carried out about cellular and mobile growth in Mexico by socio-economic levels (SEL), it can be observed that although mobile telephones are still predominant in high income sectors of the population, mobile telephone services have become a popularly used tool among low income sectors of the population. While in 2003 only 9% of the individuals in socio-economic levels D and E[5] had a mobile telephone, in 2005 that amount had tripled to 27% (Telecom CIDE, 2006).

Table 8: **Socio-Economic Level and Mobile Penetration in Mexico – 2005**

	Level A/B	Level C+	Level D+	Level D	Level E
Population distribution	10.8%	9.1%	23.8%	56.3%	
Postpaid system	28%	12%	6%	6%	4%
Prepaid system	72%	88%	94%	94%	96%
Total users (over group total)	89%	75%	67%	42%	27%

Note: The highest SEL level is "A" while "E" represents the most marginalized population sector in Mexico. Source: Telecom CIDE (2006).

---

[5] According to Mexico's SEL methodology, level "A" represents the wealthiest sector of the population, while level "E" is the poorest and most marginalized sector.

In 2005, the population segments that used the prepaid system the most were the users of SELs D and E. In addition to lower access costs, the option of having a personal device for communication offers individuals within the poorest sectors an

Figure 10: **Mobile Users under the Pre-paid Plan by Socioeconomic Level**

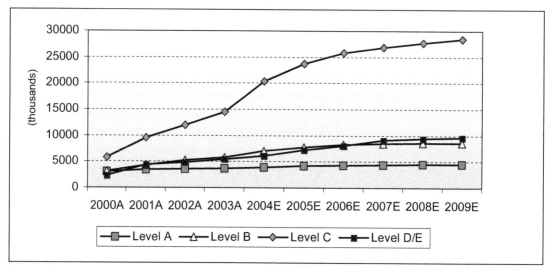

Source: Own study on projective data provided by Telefónica Movistar, Mexico.

Figure 11[6]: **Pre-paid Users by SEL 2002-2009**

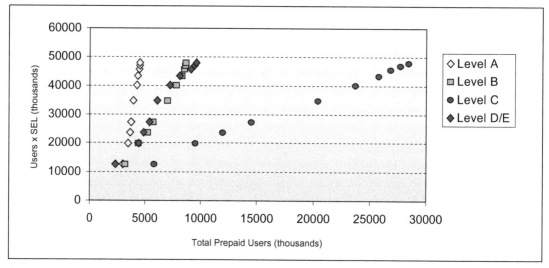

Source: Own study on projective data provided by Telefónica Movistar, Mexico.

---

[6] Figure 11 shows the relationship between the number of users according to their socio-economic level (SEL) and the total of prepaid system users over 9 years. For example, green dots indicate the number of users of SEL C and the total of prepaid system users for each year from 2000 to 2009.

independence that is not available from other types of access to communication, such as community centers, which often limit the possibility of receiving calls. The possibility to be reached should also be taken into account, since it plays a major role in terms of use, if we consider that temporary work is usually the predominant form of employment among low income sectors.

In the case of Mexico, Figures 10 and 11 show the mobile telephone contribution to servicing middle and low income groups in the country.

In all cases, the middle class, associated with socio-economic level C, will have the highest increase in total users in the coming years, compared to total prepaid system users. In addition, the time projection shows that after level C, the lowest income population sector will be the one with the highest growth in the amount of users under the prepayment plan. Thus, the prepaid system is clearly predominant and allows low income users to have access to telecommunications services, offering opportunities for using such devices as a means of payment or as the means to access other services in the future.

Regarding rural or isolated areas, due to the same payment system characteristics, but mainly due to technological, and thus cost reasons, today mobile telephony is the more viable model to respond to the demand for telecommunications services. As Navas-Sabater et al. (2002) pointed out, wireless networks offer significant cost advantages over fixed telephone services, particularly when offering services to isolated communities as well as to small towns. According to these authors, the special features provided by the mobile network (speed and ease of equipment deployment, as well as the absence of wires) make these networks a more efficient solution than fixed telephone services, especially when servicing isolated or remote communities (Navas-Savater et al., 2002).[7]

4. Conclusions

The reforms implemented in the telecommunications sectors in Latin America translated into an increase in the adoption of technology, in business efficiency and network expansion, and at the same time lowering fees. In general terms, the industry's performance today is remarkably superior. However, the task still remains of offering the benefits of modern life to society's marginalized sectors. In Latin America there are still several segments of society that do not have access to basic telecommunications services.

This task should be tackled, considering that the region is currently facing the clear presence of a regional duopoly: Telefónica Móviles and América Móvil-Telmex

---

[7] For more details, please refer to chapter 5 by Galperin and Girard, which focuses on this topic from a particular perspective.

enjoy a great and powerful position in the region. Telefónica has become the main provider of telecommunications services in most South American markets. América Móvil and Telmex have a dominant presence in Mexico and Central America and continue acquiring markets in South America. Both companies are going through deep merging and acquisition processes, making it difficult to forecast who will be the ultimate winner in the region.

What we can observe until now is that both companies have shown global survival strategies, and in some cases have sacrificed profits while fighting for their positioning in the market. As long as the Latin American market is still growing, either from unmet demand or from demand for new services, it is foreseeable that competition and not collusion will prevail. Nevertheless, it can be expected that the two companies will develop a cooperation strategy in the future. Faced with this possibility, it would be necessary to evaluate if the governments of the region should consider a region-wide regulatory strategy. This is an area for future research that should take into account economic, political and institutional differences among the Latin American countries.

Lastly, the regulatory answer to a new market context should also include the fact that mobile telephone services have become the predominant way of communication in the region. Moreover, mobile telephone services represent today an affordable means of communication for low income segments of the population. The strategies adopted by companies such as the "Calling Party Pays" program seem to have achieved more than the universal access programs carried out by the governments aiming at increasing the use of telecommunications. How should regulations encourage these types of strategies? Future research should re-evaluate the private sector's role in distributing the benefits of new information technologies to most population segments.

References

Dymond, A. & Oestman, S. (2004). The role of sector reform in achieving universal access. *Trends in Telecommunication Reform 2003*, chapter 3. Geneva: ITU.

García-Murillo, M. & Kuerbis, B. (2004). *The effects of institutional constraints on the success of universal service policies: A comparison between Latin America and the World.* Mimeo.

Gutierrez, L.H. (2003). The effects of endogenous regulation on Telecommunications expansion and efficiency in Latin America. *Journal of Regulatory Economics*, (23) 257-286.

Li, W. & Colin Xu, L. (2002). The Impact of Privatization and Competition in the Telecommunications Sector around the World. *World Bank Working Paper*, October. Washington, D.C.: The World Bank.

Mariscal, J. & Rivera, E. (2005). New trends in the Latin American telecommunications market: Telefonica & Telmex. *Telecommunications Policy*, 29(9-10), 757 777.

Navas–Savater, J., Dymond A. & Juntunen, N. (2002). Telecommunications and Information Services for the Poor: Toward a Strategy for Universal Access. The World Bank Group. *World Bank Discussion Paper No. 432.* Washington, D.C.: The World Bank.

Network Economics Consulting Group NECG. (2004).The Diffusion of Mobile Telephony in Latin America, Successes and Regulatory Challenges. Canberra: NECG.

Oestman, S. (2003). Mobile Operators: their contribution to universal service and public access. Intelecon Research. Retrieved July, 2005, from http://www.inteleconresearch.com/pdf/mobile%20&%20us%20-%20for%20rru.pdf

Shy, O. (1995). *Industrial Organization: Theory and Application.* Cambridge, MA: The MIT Press.

Stephens, R., Boyd, J. & Galarza, J. (2005). Telefonía celular: nuevo instrumento para el acceso universal en Latinoamérica. Latin.tel Regulatel, 1 (1). Retrieved April, 2005, from http://www.regulatel.org/publica/Revista/Revista.pdf

Telecom CIDE. (2006). *Contribuciones Sociales y Económicas de la Telefonía Móvil En México.* Telecom CIDE Report elaborated for Telefónica Movistar de Mexico, Mexico City, February. Available online: www.telecom.cide.edu

Wallsten, S. J. (2000). Telecommunications, Privatization in Developing Countries: The Real Effects of Exclusivity Periods. *World Bank Working Paper.* Washington, D.C.: The World Bank.

Wallsten, S. J. (2001). An Econometric Analysis of Telecom Competition, Privatization, and Regulation in Africa and Latin America. *The Journal of Industrial Economics*, 49 (1).

Wallsten, S.J. (2002). Does Sequencing Matters? Regulation and Privatization in Telecommunications Reforms. Development Research Group, The World Bank. Washington, D.C.: The World Bank.

CHAPTER 4

Institutional Design of the Regulator in Latin America and the Caribbean

Jorge Dussán Hitscherich
UNIVERSIDAD DEL ROSARIO, COLOMBIA

Juan Manuel Roldán Perea
UNIVERSIDAD DE LOS ANDES, COLOMBIA

Abstract

A direct relationship between democracy and development shows that the most fair and equal societies are the ones in which citizens have access to political and economic decision-making centers, through a legal system that guarantees the full exercise of their rights and the possibility of demanding accountability from the authorities for the trust deposited in them by the community. This is even more important when referring to poor people living in cities and rural areas. For them, the public sector – with all its structural deficits and problems – does not acknowledge their needs, and the lack of real solutions for the communities leads to an alarming and constant social tension, which affects governability in our countries. This chapter establishes the need for a change in the institutional model of the telecom regulators, aiming for more efficient regulations that address citizens' needs, especially the poorest sectors, through an increase in citizens' participation in decisions affecting them.

This chapter establishes the need of a change in the institutional model of the telecom regulator, aiming to direct the regulation more effectively to address people's needs, especially the poorest sector, through increased citizens' participation in the decisions affecting them. Unlike other chapters, this document does not refer to the institutional endowment, the relationship among the regulator and other agencies, or the description of the regulatory models that could be applied.[1] The thesis presented in this work aims at allowing consumers to participate in order to improve the regulatory system.[2] With that same purpose, a survey was designed for authorities, consumers and companies, in order to obtain statistical data to measure the effectiveness of the current mechanisms for consumer participation and the main obstacles to exercise that right. Using that information, the objective is to elaborate some recommendations that could guarantee an efficient regulatory model for consumers, in addition to revising the institutional foundations and other aspects mentioned before.

It should be taken into account that, in addition to the advantages that usually result from citizens' participation in the decisions affecting them, most of the countries in the region have already completed an initial "pro-competition" regulatory cycle, which focused on the rebalancing of tariffs, the prohibition of cross-subsidies, the privatization of trusts, the removal of entry barriers and the application of interconnection rules, among other aspects. Yet new rules need to be developed to further consumers' rights in an effective way, to reduce the risk of regulatory capture, and to make regulators aware of citizens' interests and be accountable to them for the decisions they make, prioritizing the poorest and weakest sectors.

1. Institutional Design of the Regulator

In order to support the privatization processes that took place during the last decade in almost all Latin America, telecom regulators were designed to balance investors' interests. Their purpose was to prevent capital from being caught in the usual political changes in the continent[3], and at the same time to seek the fulfillment of the

---

[1] (Levy & Spiller, 1993, p. 6).

[2] "Consumer" is not only the person who receives a service or purchases a good, but also the individual who demands the service, even when he/she is not able to purchase or receive it at a certain moment. In the telecommunications sector, it is common to identify the "consumer" with the "user" of the services. For example, the Directive 97/33/CE of the European Parliament and of the Council of 30 June, 1997 defines users as "people, including consumers, or the entities which use or request public use telecommunications services."

[3] It is worth noting, for example, that when Peru sold its state operator to Telefónica, the contract was approved by the legislative body of that country. With that action, its current owners ensured that the conditions offered would not be changed. However, it is uncommon that an act that is naturally *inter partes* is executed by a law that should be of general nature or *erga omnes*. The result is that the regulator has a very narrow margin to defend consumers, such as the application of a flat fee for Internet access or to foster competition.

following objectives: increased coverage, improved service quality and reduced fees, while directing market forces to cover the basic needs of the poorest sectors.[4]

That is how regulators have assumed that their main task is to promote competition, in order to improve service supply and improve consumers' welfare.[5] However, many sectors of the population are left outside pure market solutions. Unfortunately, the urge to continue moving on with the privatizations did not allow for a clear definition of the functions to be fulfilled by the regulatory commissions in order to solve such inequalities, nor the instruments to be used for that purpose[6]. In fact, in most Latin American and Caribbean countries, universal service policies and their financing developed after privatization and liberalization processes took place, as is shown in the following table.[7]

Table 1: **Market Reforms in Latin America**

Country	Year of Privatization	Year the Regulatory Agency was created	Year the Universal Program was created	Universal Service Fund
Argentina	1990	1996	2000	2000
Bolivia	1995	1994	2001	2001
Brazil	1998	1997	2000	2000
Chile	1988	1994	1994	1994
Colombia	NA	1994	1999	1994
Costa Rica	NA	1996	2000	2000
Ecuador	NA	1995	2000	2000
El Salvador	1998	1996	1998	1998
Guatemala	1998	1996	1996	1996
Mexico	1990	1996	2002	2002
Paraguay	NA	1995	1995	1995
Peru	1994	1994	1993	1993
Venezuela	1991	1991	2000	2000

Source: Jordana and Sancho (2000); and authors' data.

---

[4] "We have provided evidence as to the importance of Jamaica's political structure in the development of regulatory institutions and on their performance implications. A major result is that given the nature of Jamaica's parliamentary system, with a strong two-party system, with very little independence among individual members of parliament, decentralized decision making based on strong – statutory based – procedural requirements may not provide the necessary regulatory stability to promote private sector investment in sectors characterized by sunk investments and domestic consumption." Sampson & Spiller 1994, p. 53. There is also ample evidence on this issue in Stiglitz (2002).

[5] See Ariño Ortiz (2004) and Intven (2000).

[6] See Kessides (2004).

[7] It should be noted that before having a universal service policy, there was a regulation in place that ▷

On the other hand, the problem of service access by the poorest sectors, by people living in rural areas and other groups such as disabled individuals or ethnic minorities is reduced to carrying out universal access programs[8], which are designed without the participation of the people involved. Therefore, it is necessary to set up conditions to make these groups foster action on the regulator's part and become leaders to find their own solutions. In addition, the consumer relationships that arise from privatization and consolidation as markets mature, require to take into account the need for establishing wider and more effective mechanisms to protect consumers. Due to these reasons, different countries have introduced changes in their legal organizations. Some of these changes are described below.

2. The Consumer Ombudsman

If the first right of the consumers is to receive a good quality service, the second right should be to make complaints due to bad service. However, it is a mistake to think that all consumers know their rights. Although many legal systems include the possibility of making complaints about public utilities, especially about bills, a timely and adequate answer to the consumer demands is not guaranteed.

On the contrary, the numerous and dispersed rules, the lack of knowledge to use legal actions and resources, the time and effort that they demand, the difficulty to fulfill the formalities required in some cases, the number of complaints, the little amount of money the complaint may imply, the delay in the solution of the dispute, the lack of control from the authorities, and the lack of options to choose other suppliers, discourage consumers from exercising this right. Thus, it is common to observe a passive attitude in consumers, which leads to an implied authorization to forget the rules that protect them.[9]

---

forced service companies to achieve goals that benefited underprivileged sectors, e.g. to achieve a telephone density level, to install a certain number of public telephones or to provide service at affordable prices through cross-subsidies.

[8] In telecommunications, universal service programs refer to social telecommunication projects, which can be directed to "universal access" or "universal service" goals. In that sense, "universal service" is the minimum set of services, of a certain quality, available to any user, independently of his/her geographic location and, taking into account the specific national conditions, at an affordable price (Directive 2002/21/CE and Directive 2002/22/CE. It can also be found in the "Greenbook on Services of General Interest" of the Commission of the European Communities, p. 17). This set of services must be available in each household. Universal access refers to the right any person has to use a telecommunications service, initially a telephone but with the possibility of using other services such as a fax or Internet access, at a community access point. Community access projects plan one community access point for a certain population density (for example, a telephone for locations with 500 inhabitants), or an access point at a certain distance.

[9] Perez-Bustamante (2004).

Summarizing, the proliferation of mechanisms in the legal system does not guarantee consumers' rights. On the contrary, it results in tiresome proceedings and an increase in administrative and legal steps that must be taken, which represent a high burden for the State. Because of this, some countries have alternative mechanisms, such as the Ombudsman or consumer advocate, whose mission is to foster the fulfillment of the norms that govern the service and to improve the relationships between the companies and the consumers, by being involved in solving complaints, seeking the adoption of fair decisions and offering solutions in the general interest. To do so, the Ombudsman must have instruments that guarantee his/her independence, fairness and trust from the public, acting as a source of information and promoting change in the companies.[10]

According to a review of the development this mechanism has had in different countries and economic sectors, the Ombudsman or consumer advocate may have the following origin:[11]

a) **Individual Advocacy.** Created by a company to deal exclusively with matters involving them and their clients. This is the case of the Readers' or Television Viewers' Ombudsmen that has become common in the media and other industries or economic sectors such as the financial one.

b) **Joint or Decentralized Advocacy.** Created by a union or corporation; affiliated companies and their customers have access to it. This is the case of the Office of the Telecommunications Ombudsman (OTELO) in the United Kingdom, a non profit association of telecommunication services providers, including electronic communications public networks providers, public electronic communication services providers and people who offer facilities associated to a public network of electronic communications or a public service of electronic communications[12].

c) **Mixed Advocacy.** It has a legal origin, and the authorities were summoned to participate in its formation. This is the case of the Ombudsman in the Telecommunications Industry Ombudsman (TIO) in Australia, a non-government, non-profit organization made up of telephone and Internet service

---

[10] Commission of the European Communities, Recommendation 98/257/CE.

[11] Benetti Salgar (2001).

[12] OTELO reviews the complaints about services and/or products provided to residential users and small businesses under the OFCOM jurisdiction and makes sure the solutions adopted are accomplished by the telecommunications companies. Small business users are those that spend 5,000 pounds per year of service and those businesses that, in spite of spending more than 5,000 pounds per year, have 10 employees or less.

companies, as a free and independent alternative dispute resolution scheme for small business and residential consumers who have a complaint about their telephone or Internet service. In fact, what is known as TIO is a complex organization, established by the Australian Federal Government in 1993 and then acknowledged by the Telecommunications Act in 1997. It is made up of a Council, a Board of Directors and by the Telecommunications Industry Ombudsman. The Board is responsible for the administrative management, while the Council appoints the Ombudsman and designs the organization's policies and maintains its independence. The Council is made up of service provider representatives and consumer delegates. There are three more consumer delegates than industry representatives.

3. Public Hearings and Control

The citizens' participation in the management of public utilities is not limited to the advocacy of consumer rights before the companies. However, even when many countries recognize in their legislation the citizens' rights to participate in the decisions that affect them, it is very uncommon for people to become involved with the administrative responsibilities and even rarer that the officials pay attention to their opinions when making decisions.

Therefore, even when some regulators formally fulfill a process of public discussion for regulation projects, in many cases the opinions presented are not taken into account and there is nothing to force the organizations to answer the comments received. So, in practice, no advances are made regarding the disadvantages previously mentioned. Some countries, however, have improved the regulation elaboration process, clearly stating the regulator's responsibility before the consumers.

A. USA

To make a decision, the Federal Communications Commission (FCC) issues three publications (NOI or Notice of Inquiry, NPRM or Notice of Proposed Rulemaking and FNPRM or Further Notice of Proposed Rulemaking) in order to receive and review the comments of the interested parties in each opportunity. After the comments have been considered, the FCC publishes a report (R&O or Report and Order) with the new regulations, or decides not to proceed. Summaries of these reports are published in the *Federal Register*. If for any reason a person is not satisfied, he/she may submit a reconsideration request within 30 days after the day the report is issued. To answer the reconsideration request, the FCC issues a memorandum (MO&O or Memorandum Opinion and Order). If it decides to issue a regulation, it publishes a public notice (PN or Public Notice) indicating the date it intends to begin its enforcement. Many of the important regulations are decided in meetings open to the public, in which FCC commissioners discuss and vote. These meetings are announced, together with the issues to be treated, seven days in advance in the FCC's Web site.

B. CANADA

The Canadian Radio-television Telecommunications Commission communicates its intention to initiate a discussion process in its Web site and in the Canada Gazette. In addition, it may send invitations to specific groups and rural communities to participate by publishing newspaper announcements or by sending invitations with service bills, if addressed to the users.

The regulation may be discussed in a public hearing, usually when it refers to applications for new broadcasting licenses, to matters related to amendments to regulations or to a proceeding that the agency considers important. Anyone may take part in these hearings, as long as they submit their comments in writing.

C. PERU

The Organization for the Supervision of Private Investments in Telecommunications (OSIPTEL) must publish the general scope rules drafts so any interested person may participate. To do so, OSIPTEL must carry out hearings in different cities, previously announced in various media. In addition, it organizes seminars, issues publications and, in general, offers information to the public about the telecommunications sector, mainly through sharing information regarding consumers' rights through OSIPTEL's Users Management bureau, a department that assesses regulatory impact.

D. COLOMBIA

Even when the Telecommunications Regulatory Commission (CRT) was not obliged to make consultations about its regulatory projects, in 1997 the agency created an internal policy that mandated publishing on its Web site the relevant studies and drafts of the rules to be adopted, in order to receive comments from all interested parties. The presidential decree 2696 of 2004 made the CRT policy compulsory for all public utility regulators (CRA for the water and sanitation system, and CREG for the energy and gas sectors). The decree required answering the comments received and publishing a document explaining the regulator's position regarding each one of them. In addition, the regulatory commissions are forced to have a five year strategic plan and a regulatory agenda indicating the projects to be carried out each year. The draft of the agenda must be publicly discussed before its approval.

When the regulation refers to fixed telephone service fees under a special regime as residential public utility services, the CRT must present the studies based on which the fees will be set one year in advance, and partial results must also be published. Three months before the scheduled date for the fees to enter into effect, the methodology and formulas, the studies, and the texts of the resolution (with an explanatory document) must be published in the CRT web site. These documents are also sent to the Governors, who are the political-administrative heads of the second level territorial entities (departments) in order to be disseminated.

In addition, the regulatory commissions must organize public hearings in different districts and municipalities to foster users' involvement, who must be summoned 10 days in advance via different media. Hearings are recorded and a report of the discussion must be written. Public consultations, comments, information, studies and proposals made during this process are used to elaborate a document explaining the reasons for accepting or rejecting the proposals.

4. User Groups

A recent study states that the privatization of the telecommunication companies in Chile, Argentina and Brazil were the outcome of decisions made by the governments, against the people's will.[13] On the contrary, in those countries where there were public consultation processes about company privatization, such as Costa Rica and Paraguay, citizens rejected the proposal. Likewise, many Latin American consumer organizations appeared simultaneously with the privatizations of the state companies, mainly as a reaction against the increase in fees and the removal of subsidies.

---

[13] "Institutional factors such as the nature of political parties and the level of prior state organization of consumers largely determined the repertoires of contention available to consumer movements after privatization. Under the leadership of politicians and activists, Argentine consumers engaged in highly contentious collective action. They refused to pay telephone bills in protest of higher fees and organized boycotts of telephone service." Later on it adds: "The advocates of privatization generally have ignored the importance of a political voice for consumer advocacy in Latin American countries. Economic studies that do mention consumer involvement warn that any changes in policy might result in accusations that the government was retracting its commitments to business. Many political economists and business specialists seem to view the participation of consumers and consumer advocates in regulatory decisions as unnecessary politicization of technical policy arenas. Some political scientists even consider the expression of discontent through social movements to be generally disruptive and undesirable in new democracies. Others view political protest generally as a positive thing, but distrust the idea of consumer protection, or "consumerism," as a mobilizing factor.
  Most political scientists and economists, as well as politicians and policy activists, agree that new stakeholders in economic reforms must be created for such reforms to be sustained politically. Yet, while consumers would appear to be among the most obvious potential beneficiaries of reform, most analysis of privatization rarely identify consumers explicitly as political actors. Given their agreement on the importance of stakeholders, the widespread ignorance and even outright rejection of consumer-based politics on the part of policy specialists is a puzzling contradiction." (Rhodes, 2005, pp. 4–7).

It is not a coincidence that the United Nations has urged governments to adopt special policies that foster the creation of consumer organizations, to develop education and information programs for consumers and to establish quick, fair, low cost and affordable compensation mechanisms in the consumption relationships, especially for rural areas and low income sectors. According to the UN, consumer protection systems are essential to achieve a fair, equal and sustained economic and social development.[14]

Therefore, the organized participation of consumers, in addition to legitimizing the action of the authorities when duly listened to, balances the interests of all the parties in the industry, currently dominated by mega-companies present in many parts of the world.

A. USA – FEDERAL COMMUNICATIONS COMMISSION (FCC)

The Consumer Advisory Committee is part of the FCC. Its mission is to make recommendations and to facilitate the participation of consumers in proceedings before the Commission, mainly consumers living in rural areas, Native Americans and individuals with disabilities.

The Committee works mainly in the following areas:

1) Access for individuals with disabilities (for example, video description, closed captioning, readable bills, access to telecommunication products and services).

2) Consumer protection and information (for example, customer service, privacy, telemarketing abuses, services for minority groups and rural populations).

3) Implementation of consumer participation rules in the FCC ruling process.

4) Impact of the new and emerging technologies (for example, broadband availability, digital television, cable television, satellite communications, low power FM radio and the convergence of these and other new technologies).

The Committee is appointed for a period of two years and must hold meetings at least twice a year. These meetings are open to the public and must be notified in advance in the Federal Register and adequate media. Meetings are broadcast via the Internet. The FCC must provide the facilities and the human resources needed to hold the Committee meetings. The Committee members are not paid for their services, however, the FCC pays for the accommodation costs of the individuals with disabilities.

---

[14] United Nations General Assembly Resolution 39/248 of 16 April, 1985.

The Committee members are appointed by the FCC Director and the Committee Director (also appointed by the FCC Director). The members must be recognized experts in each of the fields they represent, including but not limited to consumer defense organizations, minority groups, individuals with disabilities and rural populations representatives.

B. UNITED KINGDOM – OFFICE OF COMMUNICATIONS (OFCOM)

The Communications Act of 2003 requested OFCOM to organize a Consumer Panel to give advice on matters related to consumers' interests in the market it regulates, as well as special advisory committees that represent specific interests of some groups. The Consumer Panel is completely independent, it makes public its opinions and has its own budget to carry out the research it deems adequate.

The ten members of the Consumer Panel must be appointed by OFCOM and approved by the Secretary of State. When appointing the members, OFCOM must ensure the representation of interests of each one of the nations that make up the United Kingdom. In addition, OFCOM must guarantee that the panel gives advice on issues related to the interests of the following groups:

1) People living in rural areas.

2) People living in urban areas.

3) Small businesses.

4) People with disadvantages, people on low income and disabled individuals.

5) Elderly people.

In addition to the Consumer Panel, there are advisory committees that represent the specific interests of some groups. One of them is the elderly and disabled individuals' advisory committee, made up by eleven members appointed by OFCOM.

OFCOM also has advisory committees representing the nations that make up the United Kingdom (Scotland, Northern Ireland, Wales and England). The committee members are appointed by OFCOM through a process open to the public, ensuring that the members represent the interests and opinions of the regions.

C. PERU – ORGANIZATION FOR THE SUPERVISION OF PRIVATE INVESTMENTS IN TELECOMMUNICATIONS (OSIPTEL)

In Peru, Act 28337 of July 23 2004 modified the organization of public utility regulators by adding the Users' Councils. Each regulatory agency was left to establish the structure, geographical distribution, members and proceedings to appoint or elect the members that make up the Users' Councils to ensure the effective participation of consumers and users associations, as well as the funding for the Users' Councils. The main tasks carried out by these Councils are:

1) To give opinions on the supervision, regulation, dispute resolution and answers to users' complaints, which must be carried out by the regulatory agencies.

2) To participate in public hearings.

3) To organize academic events on regulatory issues.

4) To receive and submit before the Board of Directors consultations from users regarding policies and rules of the sector.

5) To propose action plans deemed adequate to improve the quality of the services.

D. COLOMBIA – DEVELOPMENT AND SOCIAL CONTROL COMMITTEES

The Colombian Political Constitution (1991) includes the right of citizens to participate in the public services companies through the Development and Social Control Committees of Residential Public Services, made up by users or potential users of one or more public services.

The following are some of the functions the law assigns to the Development and Social Control Committees:

1) To propose to the residential public services companies plans and programs it deems necessary to solve the deficiencies in providing residential public services.

2) To try to obtain from the community the resources needed to expand or improve the residential public services, in conjunction with the residential public services companies and the municipalities.

3) To request the modification or amendment of the decisions adopted regarding residential stratification.

4) To study and analyze the amount of subsidies the municipality must offer from its budget to low income users, to examine the criteria and the distribution mechanisms of those subsidies, and to propose the measures needed for such distribution.

Each committee must choose a control member of the committee as a representative before the public services companies and the competent authorities. Some of the control member functions are to train users on their rights and to help them make their complaints to the company. In addition, control members must look after the fulfillment of the company rules and assess its operation. They have the ability to ask the authorities to take the corresponding measures and the companies are forced to answer the requests made by the control member. Control members also take part in the Board of Directors of the companies, offering solutions to solve problems and fostering corrective actions to improve its operation, especially with respect to service provision and the relationship with the public.

5. Regulator for the Poor

The direct relationship between democracy and development shows that the most fair and equal societies are the ones in which citizens have access to political and economic decision making centers, through a legal system that guarantees the full exercise of their rights and the possibility of demanding accountability from the authorities for the trust deposited in them by the community. These statements are even more important when referring to poor people living in cities and rural areas. For them, the public sector – with all its structural deficits and problems – does not acknowledge their needs, and the lack of real solutions for the communities leads to an alarming and permanent social tension, which affects governability in our countries.

Therefore, it is necessary to create legal instruments that allow any person, especially those most in need, to participate in the decisions affecting them. Traditional legal and administrative proceedings are usually inadequate, untimely, little known and difficult to use by the poor.

For that purpose, users' associations should be created with State support, and the regulatory processes should be improved, making public hearings compulsory to foster everyone's participation, with explanations suited to all education levels. Similar measures can be applied when developing projects for community access, acknowledging the reality of benefited communities and allowing them to adopt solutions and become agents of change. These projects must be designed to take into account the needs of specific groups, along with their social, economic, cultural and ethnic characteristics. Therefore, it is necessary to take into account their opinions. Unfortunately, the participation of all interested parties when elaborating these projects has not been a formal, constant or general practice. As a consequence, projects have design and execution errors, resulting in a loss of resources and efforts. In addition, it would be advisable to have a formal communication channel with the communities (e.g., Users' Committees) to assess the effects of the projects and to guide the population in the development of parallel processes (education, trade, greetings, work) in order to maximize the benefits and improve future projects.

Likewise, the possibility of introducing changes in the institutional organization of the authorities to include user representatives – as is the case in several countries with respect to television services – should be considered.[15] In this way, the prejudices against citizens' ability to responsibly discuss issues such as tariffs would be removed. In addition, it may be necessary to create new instruments to that effect, requesting that all decisions are correctly supported by studies that objectively analyze the potential impact of those decisions. These solutions may be accompanied by self-regulatory mechanisms such as the telecommunications ombudsman. Users may also be involved, and their functions may include more than just making recommendations and monitoring the policies implemented.

It is also important to have information systems that offer accurate data about users' needs and conditions, especially the poorest ones, with instruments that measure objectively the education level in relation to the service, their rights, the involvement in associations or committees, the answer given to users' complaints (including the ones resulting from service refusal), the percentage of complaints with a positive outcome, and the most frequent complaints – with a special focus on the complaints coming from the poor.

In addition, companies should be compelled to communicate the users' rights, to establish proceedings so users may make suggestions, to assess the service provided and to come up with projects to improve the service and make it available to underserved groups. These proceedings may be supervised by users through the ombudsman, the consumers' committees and the regulators, imposing sanctions on the companies when the goals set by the regulator are not met. At the same time, there must be instruments in place to preserve the neutrality of the regulators in their decisions, avoiding the risk of being captured by the industry. Thus, it is necessary that authorities clearly explain the reasons for their decisions, so they may be controlled as well.

Of course, the design of these types of institution are as difficult – or even more difficult – than the design of the regulators themselves, as many different aspects

---

[15] Only a few countries in the world have organizations to protect the freedoms and rights related to media. In Latin America such organizations exist in Argentina, Chile, Ecuador and Colombia, but only in Colombia do civil society organizations elect their members (one for the groups of parents associations and another for workers' and actors' unions, while two members are appointed by the President of the Republic and the fifth member is elected among the representatives of the television regional public channels). In Chile the members are elected by common agreement between the Executive and Legislative Branches. In the rest of the countries, the members represent state institutions. It is of significant concern that the Armed Forces are sometimes involved in those entities.

must be taken into account. Some of these aspects are the need to professionalize the individuals representing consumers, to avoid groups with other interests taking control of consumer organizations, to guarantee that democratic processes are used in their creation, and to ensure that the regulation – including companies' control – is carried out in a clear and objective manner for all parties involved. If this is achieved, policy decisions are more likely to take into account both users' interests as well as those of the investors and, above all, the general interest.

References

Ariño Ortiz, G. (2004). *Privatizaciones y Liberalizaciones en España: Balance y Resultados (Privatizations and Business Liberalizations in Spain: Balance and Outcomes) (1996-2003).* Granada: Comares.

Benetti Salgar, J. (2001). *El Arbitraje en el Derecho Colombiano (Arbitration in Colombian Law).* Bogotá: Temis.

Intven, H. (2000). Telecommunications Regulation Handbook. Washington, D.C.: *Info*Dev – The World Bank.

Jordana, J. & Sancho, D. (2000). *Reforma del Estado y Telecomunicaciones en América Latina (State Reform and Telecommunications in Latin America).* Barcelona: Universitat Pompeu Fabra.

Kessides, I. (2004). *Reforming Infrastructure - Privatization, Regulation and Competition.* Washington D.C.: The World Bank. Retrieved from http://econ.worldbank.org/prr/reforming_infrastructure/

Levy, B. & Spiller, P.T. (1993). *Regulation, Institutions and Commitment in Telecommunications: A Comparative Analysis of Five Country Studies.* Washington, D.C.: The World Bank.

Perez-Bustamante, L. (2004). *Derechos del consumidor (Consumers' Rights).* Buenos Aires: Astrea.

Rhodes, S. (2005). *Social Movements and Free-Market Capitalism in Latin America: Telecommunications Privatization and the Rise of Consumer Protest.* Manuscript.

Sampson, C.I. & Spiller, P. T. (1994). *Regulation, Institutions and Commitment: The Jamaican Telecommunications Sector.* Washington D.C.: The World Bank.

Stiglitz, J.E. (2002). *El Malestar en la Globalización (Globalization and Its Discontents).* Madrid: Taurus.

CHAPTER 5

Microtelcos in Latin America and the Caribbean

Hernan Galperin
UNIVERSIDAD DE SAN ANDRÉS/USC

Bruce Girard[1]
COMUNICA

Abstract

The problem discussed in this chapter is the failure of ICT networks and services to effectively reach the poor, particularly those living in rural areas, in Latin America and the Caribbean. The conventional answer to this problem has been to create incentives and offer public subsidies for traditional operators to cover the difference between tariffs and cost-recovery levels. This chapter examines a different answer. We suggest that microtelcos – small-scale telecom operators that combine local entrepreneurship, municipal efforts, and community action – can play an important role in extending ICT services in the region, particularly in areas unattractive to large private operators. In fact, we show that a variety of microtelcos are effectively servicing many of these areas, despite a less than favorable regulatory environment and little access to public subsidies. The chapter examines the theoretical case for microtelcos as an effective alternative to addressing the ICT needs of the poor, presents examples of microtelcos drawn from across the region, and suggests how existing regulatory obstacles for microtelcos may be removed.

---

[1] Research support was provided by Sylvia Cadena and Diego Pando. We would like to thank Francisco Proenza, François Bar and Miguel Saravia, along with our colleagues from REDIS-DIRSI, for comments on earlier drafts.

It is no longer adequate to view the provision of information and communication technology (ICT) services as a dichotomy between public utilities and large private operators. In both developed and developing nations, a diversity of organizations (among them cooperatives, municipal governments, universities and local entrepreneurs) participate in the deployment and operation of ICT networks. This is most noticeable in markets unattractive to traditional operators, where a variety of local arrangements exist to service high-cost or low-income communities. These arrangements are often hybrids of small-scale entrepreneurship, municipal efforts, and community action. What distinguishes them from traditional operators is the local scale, the use of low-cost technologies and innovative business models, and the strong community links. We refer to them as microtelcos.

The problem discussed in this chapter is the failure of ICT networks and services to effectively reach the poor, particularly those living in rural areas, in Latin America and the Caribbean. After over a decade of market-driven reforms in the telecommunications sector, it has become clear that large private operators are no more likely to serve economically unattractive areas with sparse populations or low incomes than the public operators of the past. In many countries in the region, the gap between urban and rural ICT infrastructure has increased since the onset of reforms.[2] Where networks do reach – particularly in the case of mobile telephony – coverage does not mean access since the rural poor are often unable to afford services engineered for wealthier urban customers.

The conventional answer to this problem has been to create incentives for traditional operators to service unattractive areas and offer public subsidies to cover the difference between tariffs and cost-recovery levels. While these policies have a respectable record in the developed world, the experience in Latin America is at best mixed (Estache, Manacorda, & Valletti, 2002). Efficient administration of universal service programs has proven a difficult task for the newly created industry regulators, many of which lack adequate resources (Wallsten & Clarke, 2002). Even when these programs are successful, the level of funding limits large-scale replications. It is widely acknowledged that the resources needed to address existing ICT infrastructure needs far outstrip available public subsidies in the region.

This chapter examines a different answer to this problem. We suggest that microtelcos can play an important role in extending ICT coverage in the region, particularly to high-cost or low-income areas unattractive to large private operators. In fact, we show that a variety of microtelcos are already servicing many of these areas, despite a less than favorable regulatory environment and little access to public subsidies. Their advantage lies in the mobilization of local resources, such as in-kind

---

[2] See Galperin (2005).

labor and private rights of way, as well as in the use of new low-cost technologies and innovative business models. Furthermore, much like their close cousins in water, electricity, and sanitation, microtelcos have a development impact that goes beyond the provision of services, for local ownership and management has been consistently found to spur entrepreneurship and nurture social capital (Dongier et al., 2003).

The chapter is organized as follows. In the first section we discuss the theoretical case for microtelcos as an effective alternative to address the ICT needs of the poor. Drawing from the work of Ostrom (1996) and others, we argue that there is a large scope for co-production in the delivery of ICT services between municipal government, community-based organizations (CBOs), and the private sector. Next we discuss how technological innovations are significantly enlarging the scope of action for microtelcos. We then introduce a taxonomy of microtelcos and present examples drawn from across the region. Based on the results of a regional survey of the rules governing deployment of low-cost solutions for local access networks, we argue that an enabling regulatory framework for microtelcos is lacking. We conclude with recommendations for creating such a framework.

1. The Co-production of ICT Services

Public services can be delivered in a variety of ways. For many decades, most countries relied on large state-owned utilities to provide basic infrastructure services such as electricity, water and telecommunications. A major paradigm shift took place during the last decades of the 20th century, paving the way for the privatization of many public utilities and far-reaching regulatory reforms aimed at opening markets to competition. The shift was particularly marked in the telecommunications industry, where rapid technological innovation also contributed significantly to undermine monopoly regimes.[3] It is without a question that these changes unleashed an unparalleled wave of innovation and investment in the ICT industries, first in the developed world and later in developing economies. However, after two decades of reforms the limitations of the new paradigm are now becoming clear.

It is widely recognized that large private operators are no more likely to serve high-cost or low-income customers than were state-owned utilities. This should not be surprising. Ultimately, whether in public or private hands, large utilities face similar challenges in servicing these areas: low or fluctuating incomes, low (and often decreasing) population density, lack of reliable information about customers and their demand preferences (including willingness-to-pay), lack of credit assessment mechanisms (including a formal addressing system), and lack of complementary

---

[3] There is a vast literature that documents these changes. For an overview see Noll (2000).

infrastructure (such as electricity and roads), among others. Other factors further discourage large private operators from tailoring service to the poor. The shared costs structure of telecom networks means that providing more and better services to the more profitable customers increases the cost of provision to all – even to those requiring less quality at more affordable prices. In many cases, rigid regulations on tariffs and engineering standards further discourage price/quality differentiation. Lastly, the availability of cost-based public subsidies sometimes deters large operators from seeking more efficient alternatives to serve the poor.[4]

Therefore while large private utilities are well suited for building network backbones and retailing services in wealthy urban areas, their organizational advantages tend to diminish as we approach the last-mile segment in high-cost or low-income communities. Large utilities lack either the flexibility or the incentives to seek alternative combinations of inputs better suited to serve poor customers. Microtelcos, by contrast, thrive on creative entrepreneurship. Because their core business is to serve customers unattractive to large operators, they actively seek combinations of capital, labor and technology that maximize returns based on their knowledge of local conditions and demand preferences. This involves deploying low-cost technologies, bundling ICT with related services (such as training, financial, and legal services), taking advantage of related infrastructure (such as roads and water systems), and finding business models (including payment collection mechanisms) appropriate to local conditions.

A key factor is that not all inputs necessary to optimize last-mile service delivery to the poor can be mobilized efficiently by large private utilities. Labor for infrastructure building and maintenance can often be contributed by customers themselves, often at little opportunity costs given high levels of underemployment in many poor regions. There are abundant examples of community members volunteering to set up towers, string cables, and construct facilities necessary for community network projects. It is also the case that while potential customers in these areas typically lack financial resources, they often control critical rights of way for wiring and antenna siting. Condominial lines running through household yards (and thus owned and maintained by customers themselves) have long served to extend urban sanitation networks in Brazil and Bolivia (Watson, 1995; Foster & Irusta, 2003). This is also how much of rural America was wired for telephony in the early 20th century (Fischer, 1992). Today, low-cost wireless technologies are renewing opportunities for end-user deployment and control of the first segment of the network.

---

[4] This is not the case however with smart subsidies which are increasingly used by telecom funds in Latin America and elsewhere (see Wellenius, 2001).

Municipal governments are another important actor in the provision of ICT services in these areas. In Latin America, democratic changes since the 1980s have been accompanied by decentralization programs aimed at increasing local government autonomy, creating an enabling institutional setting for the delivery of public services at the municipal level. As the examples discussed below reveal the role played by local governments in microtelco projects in Latin America varies widely (as it does elsewhere). In many cases, provincial authorities have been instrumental in aggregating demand, developing e-government applications, facilitating planning, and providing training to potential users. In other cases, municipalities have co-financed infrastructure investments through a variety of partnerships with private operators. Yet in other cases local authorities have engaged in the building and operation of a non-competitive network segment (e.g., a fiber backbone) on a wholesale basis.

Different organizations thus have a comparative advantage in each of the tasks involved in the provision of ICT services to the poor. The concept of co-production captures this well. Co-production refers to the potential complementarities that exist between different organizations in the delivery of a service (Ostrom, 1996; Gerrard, 2000). Figure 1 illustrates this potential in the delivery of broadband services. Large private operators are well positioned to build backhaul and switching facilities, though they are often reluctant to bear the risks of extending services into thin markets. Local entrepreneurs or cooperatives, by contrast, can effectively aggregate local demand, mobilize resources, develop appropriate applications, and

Figure 1: **The Co-production of Broadband Services**

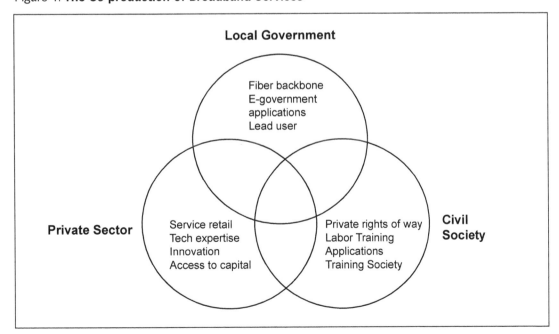

experiment with input combinations that better suit local needs. This often requires active support from local authorities to facilitate coordination, stimulate demand, and operate essential facilities.

Microtelcos are well positioned to take advantage of co-production strategies because in each case the optimal combination of inputs contributed by local government, civil society, and the private sector will vary according to local conditions. For example, condominial systems and service cooperatives are better suited in cases where strong CBOs are already present (as in the case of the Chancay-Huaral project discussed below). Municipal network projects offer an alternative when strong local institutions exist (as in the Piraí case discussed below), when fiscal revenues are decentralized, or when the municipality is already involved in the delivery of other public services. Local entrepreneurship and capital may be activated when an enabling regulatory environment is present, and when complementary services (backhaul lines and e-government application for example) are available. The most effective co-production arrangement for the provision of ICT services to the poor will thus depend on the institutional attributes of each community.

2. The Enabling Role of New Technologies

Laying telecom wires is not unlike paving roads. It requires large upfront investments, economies of scale are pervasive, and the architecture of the network has to be carefully planned in advance because resources are not easily redeployed. The process involves making many ex ante assumptions about how services will be used, by whom, and at what price. As a result, ICT networks were typically built by large operators (mostly public in the past, mostly private today) who were positioned to be able to assemble the financing and manage the risks involved in network development. Recent innovations in wireless communication and service applications are nonetheless challenging these premises. These innovations are significantly reducing the minimum efficient scale of telecom providers, allowing a variety of new actors, from small entrepreneurs to municipalities to user cooperatives, to enter the market.

A leading example is the combination of new wireless local area networking (WLAN) technologies such as Wi-Fi with wireless backbone solutions such as VSAT or the emerging WiMax standard for the provision of Internet access in remote areas.[5] Low-cost WLAN systems have been deployed by small entrepreneurs and cooperatives to service rural communities in South Asia and Latin America at a cost several orders of magnitude below that of comparable wired solutions (Best, 2003;

---

[5] For a detailed discussion of these technologies see chapter 6.

Galperin, 2005). Many small and mid-sized cities are taking advantage of these innovations to extend Internet access from a few broadband connections in government buildings to the entire community, thus lowering per user costs. Local entrepreneurs are tinkering with the technology to build point-to-point links over several kilometers to connect communities that lack adequate wired backhaul infrastructure (or to bypass links controlled by incumbents).[6]

The much flatter cost curve of WLAN technologies undermines the comparative advantages of large operators in the deployment of local networks for broadband Internet access. While upfront costs are reduced, WLAN networks are also more easily scalable or redeployed, allowing microtelcos to make modest initial investments and scale up later following demand. Instead of poles and wires, WLAN technologies take advantage of a natural resource underutilized in many poor areas: the radio spectrum. Therefore market entry is less defined by firm size than by spectrum allocation policies. Small wireless ISPs (WISPs) have flourished in countries where governments have opened frequency bands for unlicensed use, particularly in areas underserved by traditional operators.[7]

Furthermore, new mesh networking protocols are enabling the growth of condominium-style networks. This emerging architecture is based on end-users both receiving and relaying data from peer users, resulting in a network that can span a large area with only a few broadband links. This type of architecture is well suited to cases where backhaul links are scarce (and expensive), as is the case in many poor areas, as well as where the spectrum is congested, since each network node need only transmit as far as the next node (which also minimizes power requirements, another concern in many poor areas). Another advantage is robustness: when each end-user is connected to several others, multiple data routes may be available, thus bypassing failed nodes. And as more nodes are added, total network capacity grows (Benkler, 2002). While the technology is still emerging, pilot projects are already operational in Africa and elsewhere.[8]

---

[6] There are also a number of last-mile wireless alternatives, and the selection of the technology will often depend on factors such as geography, population density and services required. One promising technology used by microtelcos in Brazil and Argentina is corDECT. Developed at the Indian Institute of Technology, corDECT is a wireless local loop (WLL) technology designed to provide cost-effective, simultaneous high-quality PSTN compatible voice and high speed data connectivity for rural areas. With corDECT, rural connectivity costs are reduced from U$1,500 to about U$300 per line (Jhunjhunwala, 2000). The corDECT system is also highly modular – a single switch system can economically scale from 100 to 5,000 subscribers.

[7] In the U.S., which first allowed unlicensed operation of radio devices and today provides over 550MHz of spectrum on a license-exempt basis, there are an estimated 6,000 mom-and-pop WISPs servicing rural and other areas underserved by traditional broadband operators (FCC Wireless Broadband Access Task Force, 2005).

[8] See www.meraka.org.za for pilots in rural Africa.

New low-cost applications are having similar effects at the services layer. A leading example is Voice over IP (VoIP), which refers to a family of technologies that allow packetization and routing of voice communication over an Internet Protocol (IP) network instead of a traditional circuit-switched network. There are many advantages to IP telephony, including lower costs and more efficient use of facilities, and many large operators are migrating calls from conventional PSTN to IP networks. But the technology is particularly relevant to microtelcos because it enables provision of telephony at a fraction of the investment needed to build and maintain a traditional telephone network (Graham & Ure, 2005). Another advantage is that IP telephony is largely based on nonproprietary standards, and much of the equipment is available off-the-shelf for adaptation to local conditions.

A number of technological innovations are thus eroding the economic advantages hitherto enjoyed by large telecom operators, enabling microtelcos to extend ICT services further out into areas unattractive to conventional operators. These technologies share a number of advantages, among them lower costs, modularity based on open standards, less regulatory overhead, simple configuration and maintenance, scalability, and support for multiple applications. However, whether microtelcos and other new entrants are able to take advantage of these innovations depends to a large extent on the existence of technologically-neutral market rules, which as we shall see below is not always the case in Latin America and the Caribbean.

3. Microtelcos in Latin America: Case Studies

Critics often contend that arrangements other than large private utilities are inefficient and provide suboptimal public services (high tariffs, low quality) to the poor. In the next section we provide ample evidence to the contrary. Our findings, based on case studies from across the region that reflect different organizational arrangements, indicate that a variety of microtelcos are effectively servicing areas of little interest to traditional operators, providing affordable services and more generally acting as a catalyst for sustainable development in the communities they serve.

3.1. TELEPHONE COOPERATIVES IN ARGENTINA

A long-established model for microtelcos in Latin America and elsewhere is the telephone cooperative. This model is found for the most part in rural areas, where telephone cooperatives first emerged as the offspring of agricultural cooperatives established for various other purposes.[9] In Argentina, telephone cooperatives emerged in

---

[9] The notable exception is Bolivia, where cooperatives also service the major urban areas. The case is nonetheless atypical, for Bolivia's telephone cooperatives are not the product of organized efforts by users but were rather created by the government in 1985 to replace the incumbent municipal telephone companies (Calzada and Dávalos, 2005).

the early 1960s from efforts by local residents in areas poorly served by the former state-owned operator ENTEL. While not supported by the government, cooperatives were tolerated by ENTEL since they operated in areas considered unprofitable and brought modest revenues through tariff-sharing agreements.[10] By 1965, over 100 telephone cooperatives were operating across the Argentine territory.

When reforms began in the telecom sector in 1990, there were over 300 telephone cooperatives, many of which were part of multi-service utilities that provided electricity and water services as well. With the privatization of ENTEL, telephone cooperatives faced a period of uncertainty until 1992, when the government granted existing cooperatives a local telephony license on similar terms to those granted to the new private incumbents (which included a seven-year exclusivity period). In 1999, faced with the imminent expiration of the exclusivity period, telephone cooperatives joined forces to enter the long-distance and public telephony markets through the creation of a private subsidiary (TECOOP). By 2004, TECOOP operated approximately 230 public telephones, most of them located in remote areas.

Evaluating the performance of Argentine telephony cooperatives is difficult because of the sheer diversity of cases. Two-thirds of the cooperatives operate in small communities with fewer than 10,000 inhabitants, and the majority of them (57%) service fewer than 500 subscribers (although there are a handful of "large" cooperatives with over 5,000 subscribers). Overall, our findings indicate that telephone cooperatives have played a key role in extending basic as well as advanced ICT services outside the main urban areas. With over 600,000 subscribers, cooperatives account for about 8% of the Argentine fixed telephony market. In many of the poorest and more isolated provinces, however, their market share is much higher. In the Province of Jujuy for example, cooperative lines represent 53% of total installed lines, while in Formosa they account for 46%.

Standard measures reveal that in most cases telephone cooperatives compare favorably with traditional operators despite serving the less desirable markets. As Table 1 shows, average teledensity in the markets served by cooperatives is only moderately lower than in areas served by traditional operators (which include all major urban centers). This is remarkable if one considers that, on average (and regardless of income), a rural household in Latin America is ten times less likely than an urban one to have a telephone line.[11] In fact, if one disregards the Buenos Aires market (where the gap is higher because of the relatively high teledensity

---

[10] For much of the monopoly era (until 1990) the revenue-sharing agreement for long-distance calls between ENTEL and the cooperatives worked as follows: 60% corresponded to ENTEL, while the remaining 40% corresponded to the local cooperative.

[11] Wallsten & Clarke (2002).

Table 1: **Teledensity in Cooperative Territories vs. Total Teledensity, 1998**

Province	Population in cooperative	Cooperative subscribers territories	Teledensity (A)	Total Province Teledensity (B)	(B-A)
Buenos Aires	686,736	109,568	16.0	22.0	−6.0
Catamarca	36,939	2,399	6.5	9.1	−2.6
Chaco	25,000	1,658	6.7	7.2	−0.5
Chubut	9,700	1,679	17.3	19.8	−2.5
Córdoba	183,950	27,837	15.1	18.4	−3.3
Formosa	82,000	8,472	10.3	4.5	5.8
Jujuy	146,000	11,285	7.7	6.3	1.4
La Pampa	7,265	1,493	20.6	19.4	1.2
Neuquén	128,000	18,884	14.8	13.4	1.4
Río Negro	25,200	2,547	10.1	15.9	−5.8
San Luis	39,980	5,251	13.1	13.5	−0.4
Santa Cruz	59,100	8,966	15.2	14.2	1.0
Santa Fe	268,054	41,813	15.6	18.9	−3.3
Total	**1,698,284**	**241,852**	**14.2**	**19.2**	**−5.0**
Total w/o Buenos Aires	**1,011,548**	**132,284**	**13.1**	**15.5**	**−2.4**

Source: Secretaría de Comunicaciones (SECOM).

around the capital city), the difference in teledensity between the areas served by the incumbents and the areas served by the cooperatives is relatively small.

Our case studies also reveal that average prices for services provided by cooperatives tend to be similar or lower than those of large operators. In fixed telephony services, average connection costs are 32% lower for cooperatives. Prices for dial-up Internet access services are comparable with those of larger operators, despite higher provision costs due to lack of competitive leased lines in rural areas (nonetheless prices for xDSL services were found to be significantly higher). Part of the cost advantage is explained by faster technological adoption. Motivated by the need to service customers in low-density areas at the lowest possible cost, cooperatives are constantly seeking lower-cost technologies appropriate for their business models. Telpin, a cooperative in a relatively wealthy community south of Buenos Aires, installed the first digital exchange in Argentina in the early 1980s, which enabled provision of a host of value-added services which the incumbent only offered after privatization (Finquelievich & Kisilevsky, 2005).

Cooperatives have also pioneered wireless last-mile and backhaul solutions. Local loop systems based on corDECT have been deployed by cooperatives in the provinces of Chubut, Neuquen, and Cordoba, allowing fast network roll-out at a fraction of the cost of traditional copper. Wi-Fi has been the technology of choice for many cooperatives providing broadband Internet access services. Cooperatives have also been eager to enter the wireless telephony market, since competition from wireless carriers has significantly affected revenue growth. The main effort is centered around the acquisition of a national wireless license through Comarcoop, a joint venture formed by several telephony and electricity cooperatives. There are also more localized efforts such as that of CoTeCal, a telephone cooperative in the remote Patagonian city of El Calafate, which has partnered with Chinese electronics giant Huawei and the provincial government to test CDMA450, a third-generation cellular telephony system better suited to service sparsely-populated areas than traditional PCS systems.[12]

It is also important to acknowledge the spillover benefits to the community as a whole associated with the telephone cooperative model. Our findings indicate that cooperatives have a significant involvement in ICT training and dissemination activities (which also serve to boost demand for value-added services), while many cooperatives have also engaged in local content development (typically community portals) in association with various CBOs and local governments. Despite the lack of subsidy payments from the government, many cooperatives set special tariffs for low-income residents while others provide free services (particularly Internet access) to public schools and libraries. Finally, telephone cooperatives promote local capacity building and nurture community solidarity, two important ingredients long identified by development scholars as critical for empowering the poor (Birchall, 2003).

3.2. WIRELESS COMMUNITY NETWORKS IN PERU

Recently, a number of microtelcos have emerged from existing CBOs created for purposes other than the provision of ICT services. A project in the Chancay-Huaral valley of Peru illustrates this deployment and ownership model. The Chancay-Huaral river irrigates a large area of small-scale farming (95% of farms have less than 10 hectares of land) on the sides of the valley. While the area has potential wealth due to its good land, abundant water and proximity to the markets of Lima and the north of the country, farmers have not been able to adapt their production to the fluctuations of the agricultural markets. Additionally the inhabitants of the valley have little or no access to public services and the communications infrastructure available to them is at best precarious.

---

[12] CDMA450 works on a lower frequency band (450MHz), and thus requires considerably fewer towers to cover an extensive area.

CEPES, a Peruvian NGO, reasoned that there was a connection between the lack of communication and services and the fact that farmers tended to grow the same crops regardless of market prices. They also noted that the lack of communications created problems for the efficient management of the waters of the river Huaral, a common resource used by the valley's farmers and managed by the Water Users Board, a cooperative organization of the seventeen Irrigation Commissions spread throughout the valley (which are in turn composed of farmers themselves, about 6,000 in total). To address these problems, CEPES proposed to establish an agricultural information and communication system for the valley, providing farmers with training and access to information that would enable them to make better decisions, and facilitating communication among the irrigation commissions to improve water management. Because the available communications infrastructure was inadequate, a Wi-Fi network was deployed joining twelve villages in the valley and connecting them to the Internet through a shared 512 Kbps line and a VSAT link.

The desertification of Peru's coastal areas is a serious problem, and thus the local Irrigation Commission, which manages irrigation and other uses of water, is one of the most important CBOs for communities along the Chancay-Huaral valley. While the project was initiated by CEPES and funded by Peru's telecom development fund (FITEL), the Chancay-Huaral Water Users Board was selected as the owner/operator of the network because of its experience in managing infrastructure, its close contact with local farmers, and the presence of the Irrigation Commissions in each of the valley's villages. Beyond infrastructure deployment, the project emphasized the development and maintenance of a database of agricultural information, the training of farmers in the effective use of agricultural information, and the strengthening of local capacity for obtaining, distributing and using agricultural information.

As the project became operational, it also evolved to better meet local demand for ICT services. IP telephony quickly took on a central importance, not only for linking the local Irrigation Commissions and the Board but also for general use by local residents. Providing access to other local residents (beyond farmers themselves) also became a priority. Since available bandwidth far exceeds the needs of the Irrigation Commissions, a number of local institutions such as schools were invited to join the network. The Board is currently working to extend connectivity for other CBOs, public offices, and private entities, as well as to set up telecenters for the public at large.

While not immediately replicable, the Chancay-Huaral project illustrates a number of the advantages of the CBO-driven microtelco model. The adoption of IP telephony and the scaling of the network reveals the ability to rapidly adapt to community needs. While the decision to provide connectivity to other institutions and individuals stems in part from an interest to contribute to community development, it is also part of a sustainability plan based on cost-sharing by public, private, and civil society partners. Inter-local cooperation has also been critical, for each village is responsible for local network maintenance, with training provided by CEPES. In addition, new WLAN technologies have allowed flexibility in terms of service provision and scaling of the network with a modest initial investment.[13]

3.3. MUNICIPAL NETWORKS IN BRAZIL AND ARGENTINA

Municipal network projects have attracted much publicity (both good and bad) as of late.[14] Many question local government involvement in the provision of ICT services as the new face of the old state-utility model, noting its poor record of service quality, innovation, and network extension. Yet a closer look reveals significant differences. To begin with, the new breed of projects is led by local rather than national authorities. Under the right circumstances, the delivery of public services has been recognized to be more effectively organized at the local level (Azfar & Cadwell, 2003). Municipal network projects often start from this principle, delivering services tailored to local needs and integrating ICT with broader economic and social development activities.

This is the case of Piraí, a rural municipality of about 25,000 inhabitants in the State of Rio de Janeiro, Brazil. The Piraí Digital project was started in the late 1990s when the municipality received a small grant from the Federal Government to modernize its local tax office. At the time, the entire local government ran on two phone lines and two computers. While part of these resources were earmarked for a hybrid fixed-wireless IP network to connect different government offices, local authorities realized that broadband connectivity could be extended to a much larger area at little extra cost. A community committee was then formed, which included municipal authorities and representatives from CBOs and the private sector, to chart a more ambitious plan that would extend wireless connectivity to much of the Piraí territory. The project was conceived as the cornerstone of a broader plan to diversify the local economy and attract new investments following privatization

---

[13] The initial investment reached US$33,600, or about US$2,800 per village.

[14] It is important to distinguish municipal *networks* from municipal *e-government* initiatives. Broadly speaking, municipal e-government concerns the provision of local government services over an existing network platform provided by third parties, as well as the use of ICT to improve internal government operations. By contrast, our attention is on municipal network projects where the local government is involved – in a variety of different ways – in infrastructure roll-out and the delivery of ICT services to the public.

(with significant layoffs) of the state-owned power utility, then the largest local employer.

The community committee proved critical in securing partnerships with universities, NGOs, and private firms, which contributed to the project with equipment, application development, and expertise in the deployment and operation of the municipal network. The project focused on four areas: e-government (the original remit of the initiative), education (including distance education in partnership with a consortium of public universities), public access points (including training in partnership with various NGOs) and SME adoption. To date, the network has over 50 broadband nodes, connecting all local government offices and most of the public schools and libraries. There is also a growing number of public access points, and a private company with majority municipal ownership has been formed to commercialize services to households and businesses.

The lessons from the Piraí case point to several success factors. First, the lack of public subsidies (beyond the small grant to modernize the tax office) forced community leaders to draw in resources through cooperation with a variety of actors from the private and civil society sectors (both local and otherwise). Inputs were thus assembled through a combination of in-kind contributions, partnerships, and the city's modest budget. Second, the use of low-cost technologies at the transport (i.e., WLAN) and terminal (i.e., open-source software) layers dramatically reduced upfront costs, allowing Piraí to provide broadband services where traditional cable and xDSL operators could not justify investments.[15] Finally, local leadership, good governance and strong social capital enabled collective planning and management of the project, contributing to better match services with local needs.

The case for municipal networks is stronger when the local government is already providing other public services (e.g., electricity and sanitation), since economies of scope often allow provision of ICT services at minimal extra costs. A good example is the SICOMU (Sistema de Comunicaciones Multimediales) initiative in the Argentine province of La Pampa. This case illustrates the combination of market failures, economies of scope, and internal needs that often drive the municipal microtelco model. The project began as an appendix to the construction of a large aqueduct undertaken by the provincial government. Having contracted for over 1,300 kilometers of aqueduct building and secured the necessary rights of ways, provincial authorities decided to lay telecom fiber alongside the aqueduct.

The network was initially conceived as an Intranet that would support the internal control systems for the operation of the aqueduct. However it soon became

---

[15] According to estimates by Franklin Dias Coelho, general project coordinator of Piraí Digital, the city was able to reduce deployment and operation costs by a factor of eight (personal interview).

evident that excess capacity could be utilized to service municipalities along the aqueduct route with minimal incremental investments in feeder lines. The provincial government thus enlisted 21 municipalities to participate in the project, most of them rural communities with few other connectivity alternatives. While the provincial government operates the network backbone (the fiber along the aqueduct and feeder lines), each of the municipalities is responsible for extending the network to local government offices, hospitals, schools and public libraries, as well as selecting and managing the services provided at the local level (which range from e-government applications to IP telephony).

Other local actors also provide important complementary assets. The local university (Universidad Nacional de La Pampa) is utilizing the network for a variety of distance education initiatives (the university's only campus is located in the provincial capital of Santa Rosa). The local branch of the National Institute for Agricultural Technology (INTA) has made available online consultation and support services to local farmers. In addition, about half of the total network capacity is being offered as dark fiber to third parties for the commercialization of services in all or parts of the network. This is expected to offset a substantial part of the operating costs of the project. Local electricity cooperatives have already contracted to begin offering telephony services.

Whereas the public utilities of the past financed, built, and operated the entire network, municipal ICT projects today are more likely characterized by different degrees of cooperation with the private sector, CBOs, and other organizations (oftentimes educational institutions). Our findings indicate that municipal network projects aim at facilitating investments in underserved areas rather than competing with established operators. They also suggest how, as one of the largest users of ICT services in the community, local governments benefit from financing and/or managing their own infrastructure where private operators fail to invest adequately. Many municipal networks have emerged from the need to equip local government offices and public entities (schools, libraries, police stations, health centers, etc.) with better ICT access, later evolving into broader initiatives that service local businesses and residents. While further research is needed, preliminary findings suggest that both municipal and provincial authorities have an array of roles to play in spurring ICT development at the local level.

3.4. SMALL PRIVATE OPERATORS IN COLOMBIA

While Colombia is among the few nations in the regions that have not fully privatized its legacy operators, the liberalization of the telecommunications market in 1994 has resulted in significant private investments in the sector. A large part of these investments has flowed into mobile telephony as well as into the legacy municipal operators, which have been privatized to varying degrees (Telecom, the national operator, remains public).[16] Yet market reforms have also resulted in the emergence of a number of small private operators, many of them serving areas poorly served by the incumbents. While some of these operators are affiliates of larger firms with presence in various local markets, others are the product of independent efforts by small entrepreneurs who bear the majority of the risks themselves.

The evidence suggests that small-scale private operators are gaining ground in the Colombian market. As the total number of fixed lines roughly doubled between 1994 and 2002, the number of lines controlled by small operators more than tripled in the same period, increasing their share from 7% in 1994 to 11% in 2002.[17] The available data also reveals that small-scale operators compare favorably with larger firms on standard quality measures. The Quality Index computed by the Colombian regulator (which is factored into price regulations) reveals that small operators consistently outperform larger operators as measured by traditional quality indicators (faults per 100 lines, average days to obtain new connection, average days to repair a faulty line) as well as subscriber satisfaction surveys.[18]

Small private operators nonetheless still face a myriad of challenges, even when serving areas neglected by incumbents, which the case of TELEOCSA illustrates well. The birth of TELEOCSA dates back to the early 1990s when a group of community leaders from Puente Piedra, a small town near the capital city of Bogotá, approached the national operator (Telecom) to request the extension of local telephony services to the community. Lacking the capital and the incentives to fulfill the request, Telecom instead proposed to community leaders that local residents purchase the equipment (including switches and cabling), deploy the network, and later transfer ownership of all facilities to Telecom, which would then operate the network and provide interconnection with its long-distance lines.

Lacking alternatives, community leaders agreed to these terms and the project

---

[16] For further details see Uribe Botero (2005).

[17] Source: CRT.

[18] In 2001 for example, the average Quality Index score (on a 100-point scale) for small operators was 90.1, compared to 89.4 for medium-size operators and 87 for large operators. Source: authors' own calculations based on CRT (2002).

was started soon after. With the passing of the new telecommunications law in 1994 that allowed unrestricted private sector participation in the provision of local telephony, community leaders changed course and decided to create a private local operator rather than transfer ownership to Telecom. A year later, TELEOCSA was incorporated and obtained a local operator license. What ensued was a protracted regulatory battle between the new company and the incumbent, which not only refused to interconnect but asserted ownership over TELEOCSA's facilities, even when the totality of the investment was borne by local residents. At its peak in 2002 TELEOCSA had 1,200 subscribers, but after several unsuccessful attempts to obtain interconnection with Telecom's long-distance network the project was folded in November 2004.

This case illustrates the need for a vigilant regulator to protect new entrants from anti-competitive strategies by the incumbents in control of higher-level facilities. While this is the case for any new entrant, it is particularly important for the emergence and survival of microtelcos, which cannot bargain effectively with incumbents and typically lack the resources or expertise to wage lengthy regulatory or judicial battles. The next section discusses this and other regulatory obstacles faced by microtelcos.

4. The Need for an Enabling Regulatory Environment

Regulatory constraints have long been a major barrier to entry in the ICT markets of Latin America and the Caribbean. Despite ongoing reforms, our findings indicate that microtelcos face a myriad of regulatory barriers that discourage entry, limit scalability and constrain experimentation with new technologies and business models better suited to service high-cost/low-income areas.

Spectrum access. Our case studies suggest that Wi-Fi and other WLAN technologies represent key enabling technologies for microtelcos, having been deployed to provide a variety of services (from broadband Internet access to VoIP) in different social and geographic contexts. This is however premised on the availability of the frequency bands in which these technologies operate (2.4GHz and 5GHz). International experience reveals that spectrum policies that provide for unlicensed access to these bands empower microtelcos by facilitating rapid infrastructure deployment without the lengthy administrative procedures traditionally associated with wireless networks (Galperin & Bar, 2004).

In recent years, countries in the Latin American and Caribbean region have been reforming spectrum administration to allow for increased unlicensed use by low-power devices (such as Wi-Fi radios) in these bands. However, our findings from a survey of 25 countries in the region reveal that significant roadblocks persist.[19] The vast majority (82%) of the countries in the region have taken steps to allow for unlicensed WLAN deployment in the 2.4GHz band, though about a third of them still require public access points to be registered with the telecom authority. While this is encouraging, in many countries power restrictions significantly limit outdoors deployment opportunities (and thus the appeal of the technology for new service providers). Overall, a third of the countries have set power limits below 1W (the FCC standard), thus limiting the potential reach of Wi-Fi signals to a few hundred meters at best (although in certain cases such as Brazil and Peru exceptions are made for the less populated areas).[20]

In the 5GHz band, the situation is less encouraging. About two-thirds of the countries (68%) allow unlicensed operation in the upper portion of the band (5.725-5.850MHz), and of those 40% require equipment registration with the telecom authorities. Moreover, of the countries where unlicensed use is authorized, 40% of them restrict power below 1W (the FCC standard).[21] In the lower portion of the band (5.150-5.350MHz), only about a third (35%) of the countries in the region authorize unlicensed use in these frequencies, and in most of these cases operation is limited to indoor spaces.[22] Finally, only Brazil, Panama and Colombia have so far authorized unlicensed use in the middle portion of the 5GHz band (5.470-5.725MHz). Although this is expected to change in the medium term as these frequencies have only recently been designated by the ITU for WLAN devices, there are less encouraging cases such as Mexico where telecom authorities have recently designated the band for licensed use exclusively.

Licensing. Licensing rules often discriminate against microtelcos, either implicitly by requiring lengthy administrative procedures that microtelcos are unable to navigate, or explicitly by preventing non-traditional operators from controlling network components or supplying services. As an example, telephone cooperatives in Argentina are legally barred from offering broadcasting and other complementary services, thus preventing bundling strategies. In Peru, the Chancay-Huaral project discussed above was prevented from terminating voice calls in the PSTN because of

---

[19] The database is available from the authors upon request. It will also be available through www.wilac.net.

[20] In Brazil for example, the power limit is set at 400mW for areas with more than 500,000 inhabitants, rising to 1W for areas below 500,000.

[21] These power restrictions represent an even more serious constraint for service providers because of the propagation characteristics of radio signals at 5GHz.

[22] While indoor-only use is the international norm in the 5.150-5.250MHz portion of the lower 5GHz band, many countries allow for outdoor use in the 5.250-5.350MHz range.

the lack of a telecom operator license (obtaining such a license entails a lengthy administrative procedure which also triggers a number of financial obligations, including a contribution of 1% of operating revenues to the Peruvian telecommunications development fund). It is nonetheless encouraging that many nations are moving towards a differentiated licensing regime with less burdensome requirements for rural and underserved areas (this is the case of Peru and Argentina, among others).

Lack of technological neutrality. In the name of consumer protection, ICT services are sometimes subject to overly strict quality of service and engineering standards that preclude microtelcos from deploying low-cost solutions. This discourages seeking price/quality combinations better suited for the poor, and reduces opportunities for bypassing essential facilities controlled by incumbents. The case of VoIP is illustrative. Our survey of 18 countries in the region found that less than half of them (38%) have authorized the use of IP networks to provide telephony services. Interestingly, only a handful explicitly prohibit the use of VoIP: in most cases, the technology is in a legal limbo, neither completely legal nor illegal.

This has not prevented many local entrepreneurs from offering VoIP services. In most countries in the region, telecenter operators offer long-distance calls over broadband connections at a fraction of the cost of incumbent carriers. Analysts estimate that Latin America accounts for 35% of global VoIP traffic (compared to 9% of PSTN).[23] Yet lack of legal protection has discouraged further investments, and reports of government crackdowns on establishments and firms offering VoIP services on the grey market are not uncommon.

Another illustrative case are the service restrictions placed on the use of WLAN technologies. As discussed, in several cases the use of WLAN technologies is restricted to indoor spaces or private use, thus reducing the value of WLAN solutions as a last-mile access alternative for microtelcos. This was the case, until recently, of the 2.4GHz band in Peru, which required the Water Users Board in Chancay-Huaral to seek a special waiver from OSIPTEL (the Peruvian regulator) to deploy its network (the rules have since then been modified to allow outdoors deployment in underserved areas). There are also cases in which specific services are prohibited, such as in Argentina where regulators have recently prohibited the supply of telephony services over WLANs in the major metropolitan areas. As innovations continue to enhance the reach and capacity of wireless solutions, incumbents will attempt to seek protection against disruptive technologies, which will require increased regulatory vigilance to accepted principles of technological neutrality.

---

[23] Source: Telegeography (2004).

Lack of financing. For traditional carriers servicing poor or distant communities, subsidy payments are often available through universal service and telecom development funds. In some cases, the administration of these funds discriminates against microtelcos by aggregating targeted areas and centralizing project management functions. The unintended result is that only large operators with a regional or national presence are able to compete for funds. This was for example the case of the Compartel program in Colombia, where in 1999 a large contract for the development of community telecenters was split between Gilat (670 telecenters) and Telefónica (270 telecenters). While this reduces administrative costs, it also jeopardizes long-term sustainability since services are dependent on the availability of external subsidies and unresponsive to local needs. Centralized projects are also more vulnerable to political patronage, as was the case with the failed CTC initiative in Argentina (Galperin, 2005).

Access to essential facilities. The provision of telecommunications services at the local level requires access to switching facilities and trunk lines often controlled by incumbent operators. Like many other new entrants, microtelcos often face discriminatory access to these facilities. While Latin American regulators are increasingly engaged in the oversight of interconnection contracts between incumbents and new entrants, their limited resources pose challenges to effective implementation. For example, a recent study found that few nations in the region provide guidance to the pricing and interconnection arrangements between incumbents and new entrants in the provision of broadband Internet access services (Regulatel, 2005). Lack of regulatory attention to issues of non-discriminatory access to essential facilities discourages entry by increasing the risks associated with last-mile infrastructure deployment. This is well illustrated in the case of TELEOCSA.

5. Conclusions

Market reforms in the ICT sector in Latin America and the Caribbean have not paid sufficient attention to the important role that microtelcos play in the supply of services in thin markets outside the main urban centers. These operators have been found to provide services comparable to those of traditional operators in high-cost/low-income areas with minimal public subsidies. They do so through a variety of innovative business and co-production strategies, combining inputs from local entrepreneurs, municipal authorities, and CBOs to address ICT needs in markets considered unprofitable by traditional operators.

One of the main advantages of microtelcos is their ability to adopt the technologies and business models best suited to serve local residents at different price/quality points. A variety of local conditions determine the optimal organization and combination of inputs for microtelcos, including the economic and social profile of the community, geographic factors (terrain, distance to urban centers, etc.) and the structure of the overall telecom market. However, our findings reveal that institutional factors are also critical. When good local governance exists (as in the Piraí case), municipal networks offer a promising alternative for spurring network roll-out. When strong CBOs are present (as in the Chancay-Huaral case), microtelco projects may benefit from building upon their integration into the economic and social fabric of the community. In many cases local resources and entrepreneurship can be effectively activated (as in the TELEOCSA case), but this requires active regulatory support to prevent anti-competitive maneuvering by the incumbents.

Overall, our findings suggest that a level playing field for microtelcos is lacking. There is however encouraging evidence that the regulatory mood is changing. Principles such as technological neutrality, open access to essential facilities, and a public good rationale in certain ICT network components are beginning to take hold. Several nations have loosened licensing, spectrum access and tariff regulations to stimulate telecom investments in rural areas. There is also increasing recognition among policymakers that, alongside with private operators, public–private-CBO partnerships have an important role to play in extending networks and services to the rural poor. Finally, universal access programs in many nations now provide support for microtelco projects alongside large-scale subsidy schemes. Our findings provide support for these second generation reforms that acknowledge the diversification of ICT supply and community development spillovers as important principles in the design and implementation of ICT policies in the region.

References

Azfar, O. & Cadwell, C. (Eds). (2003). *Market-augmenting Government: The Institutional Foundations for Prosperity.* Ann Arbor: University of Michigan Press.

Bar, F. & Galperin, H. (2004). Building the Wireless Internet Infrastructure: From cordless Ethernet archipelagos to wireless grids. *Communications and Strategies, 54*(2), 45-68.

Benkler, Y. (2002). Some Economics of Wireless Networks. *Harvard Journal of Law and Technology, 16*(1), 25-83.

Best, M. (2003). The wireless Revolution and Universal Access. In *Trends in Telecommunications Reform.* Geneva: ITU.

Birchall, J. (2003). *Poverty Reduction through Self-help: Rediscovering the cooperative advantage.* Geneva: International Labour Organisation (ILO).

Calzada, J. & Dávalos, A. (2005). Cooperatives in Bolivia: Customer ownership of the local loop. *Telecommunications Policy, 29*, 387-407.

Comisión de Regulación de Telecomunicaciones. (2002). *El sector de las telecomunicaciones en Colombia.* Bogota: CRT.

Dongier, P., Van Domelen, J., Ostrom, E., Ryan, A., Wakeman, W., Bebbington, A., Alkire, S., Esmail, T., & Polski, M. (2003). Community-driven Development. In *World Bank Poverty Reduction Strategy Paper.* Washington, DC: The World Bank.

Estache, A., Manacorda, M., & Valletti, T. (2002). Telecommunications Reforms, Access Regulation, and Internet Adoption in Latin America. *Economica, 2*, 153-217.

Federal Communications Commission. (2005). *Wireless Broadband Access Task Force report.* Washington, DC: FCC.

Finquelievich, S., & Kisilevsky, G. (2005). Community Democratization of Telecommunications Community Cooperatives in Argentina: The case of TELPIN. *The Journal of Community Informatics, 1*(3), 27-40.

Fischer, C. (1992). *America Calling: A social history of the telephone to 1940.* Berkeley: University of California Press.

Foster, V. & Irusta, O. (2003). *Does Infrastructure Reform Work for the Poor? A case study on the cities of La Paz and El Alto in Bolivia.* World Bank Policy Research Working Paper No. 3177. Washington, DC: The World Bank.

Galperin, H. (2005). Wireless Networks and Rural Development: Opportunities for Latin America. *Information Technologies and International Development, 2*(3), 47-56.

Gerrard, C. (2000). *Ten Institutionalist Perspectives on Agricultural and Rural Development.* Presented at the IAAE Conference, Berlin.

Graham, T. & Ure, J. (2005). IP Telephony and Voice over Broadband. *Info, 7*(4), 8-20.

Jhunjhunwala, A. (2000). *Unleashing Telecom and Internet in India.* Presented at the India Telecom Conference, Stanford University.

Noll, R. (2000). Telecommunications Reform in Developing Countries. In A.O. Krueger (Ed.), *Economic Policy Reform: The Second Stage.* Chicago: University of Chicago Press.

Ó Siochrú, S. & Girard B. (2005). *Community-based Networks and Innovative Technologies: New models to serve and empower the poor.* New York: UNDP

Ostrom, E. (1996). Crossing the Great Divide: Co-production, synergy, and development. *World Development, 24*(6), 1073-1087.

Regulatel. (2005). La Banda Ancha en el Ámbito de Regulatel. Mimeo.

Saravia, M. (2005) Rural Telecommunications Networks in Peru. In *Community-based Networks and Innovative Technologies*, Ó Siochrú & Girard. New York: UNDP.

Uribe Botero, E. (2005). *Evolución del Servicio de Telecomunicaciones Durante la Última Década*. Documento CEDE 2005-23. Bogota: Universidad de los Andes.

Wallsten, S. & Clarke, G. (2002). *Universal(ly bad) Service: Providing infrastructure services to rural and poor urban consumers*. Policy Research Working Paper Series 2868. Washington, DC: The World Bank.

Watson, G. (1995). *Good Sewers Cheap?* UNDP/World Bank Water & Sanitation Program. Washington, DC: The World Bank.

Wellenius, B. (2001). *Closing the Gap in Access to Rural Communication: Chile 1995–2002*. Washington, DC: The World Bank.

CHAPTER 6

Selecting Sustainable ICT Solutions for Pro-poor Intervention

Kim I. Mallalieu and Sean Rocke[1]

DEPARTMENT OF ELECTRICAL AND COMPUTER ENGINEERING
THE UNIVERSITY OF THE WEST INDIES, ST. AUGUSTINE, TRINIDAD AND TOBAGO

Abstract

This chapter describes a Percolator model as a framework within which ICT solutions may be contemplated for communities under threat of digital exclusion. The model partitions the problem into manageable domains, within which realistic and appropriate ICT solutions may be progressively distilled. It gives an account of the generic attributes of information and communications and the manner in which these attributes map onto technical parameters of ICT. The model places a great deal of emphasis on contextualization, drawing on the Sustainable Livelihood Approach for intervention in economically poor communities. Its domains variously take account of the national or provincial developmental objectives in specific politico-cultural contexts as well as the social character of communities and their physical nature. Ultimately, contextualized technical parameters are used as the basis on which solutions are selected from among the available range of information and communications technologies. The general framework of the Percolator model is not limited to ICT. It may be applied to intervention based on a variety of technologies.

[1] The authors acknowledge, with gratitude, the contribution of Akash Pooransingh in the acquisition of supporting resources for this work.

ICTs have been inextricably linked to social development (UNDP, 1996; UNDP, 1999; G-8, 2000; DFID, 2002; World Bank, 1999; Cecchini & Shah, 2002). Yet there are poles of opinion regarding the application of these technologies in communities for which they find no natural or ready home. Many authors have analyzed the fundamental as well as the practical sources of failure in these communities (Avgerou, 2000) while many have reported on their tremendous successes. Indeed, the deployment of ICT in digitally impoverished communities by digitally privileged ones is fraught with pitfalls, most particularly when they are contemplated as an a priori solution to general or ill defined problems, with little regard for communities' cultural, social and physical nature.

History has shown that ICT can enable the realization of social developmental objectives to the extent that they can enable appropriate and long-lasting lifestyle changes. It is imperative, therefore, that ICT-based intervention takes account, not only of the technologies themselves, but also of the ultimate developmental objectives and, very importantly, of the many factors which impact on sustainability.

We posit that there are fundamental principles which underlie the success of ICT intervention by external agents, namely that:

1. Such intervention must be ultimately driven by general developmental objectives as articulated by national or provincial policy.

2. These ultimate developmental objectives may only be achieved through the parallel engagement of many sectors.

3. ICT is one such sector.

We further posit that successful ICT-based intervention is:

- Driven from the bottom as well as from the top

- Structured according to independent but interacting domains

Based on these fundamental principles, the authors have developed a framework for the contemplation of ICT solutions for digitally poor communities which, as Barrantes' chapter in this book demonstrates, are not restricted to communities that are economically poor.

Recognizing the essential multi-disciplinary, multi-sectoral nature of development and the vast and multi-faceted nature of the proposition of intervention, the framework is partitioned into component domains. Application of the framework draws upon a number of existing analytical as well as operational tools.

1. The Percolator Model

The authors define a "Percolator model" as a framework to guide the selection of technological intervention solutions for communities of interest. This Percolator model is illustrated for ICT-based intervention in Figure 1. It comprises three domains: the broad contextual or "Base" Domain, the User Domain and the Technology Domain. The Base Domain loosely defines the scope of livelihoods which are compatible with national or provincial developmental objectives and are at the same time realistic in a particular political and cultural setting. The User Domain defines technical requirements that derive from the attributes ascribed to information and communications in the context of traditions of abilities and inter-action as well as from sectoral objectives, where such exist. The Technology Domain defines the set of ICT solutions, from amongst the available set of information and communications technologies, which are well suited to the physical con-text of particular communities and which are constrained by the technical require-ments that have percolated up the two underlying domains.

Figure 1: **Percolator Model for Contemplating ICT Intervention Solutions**

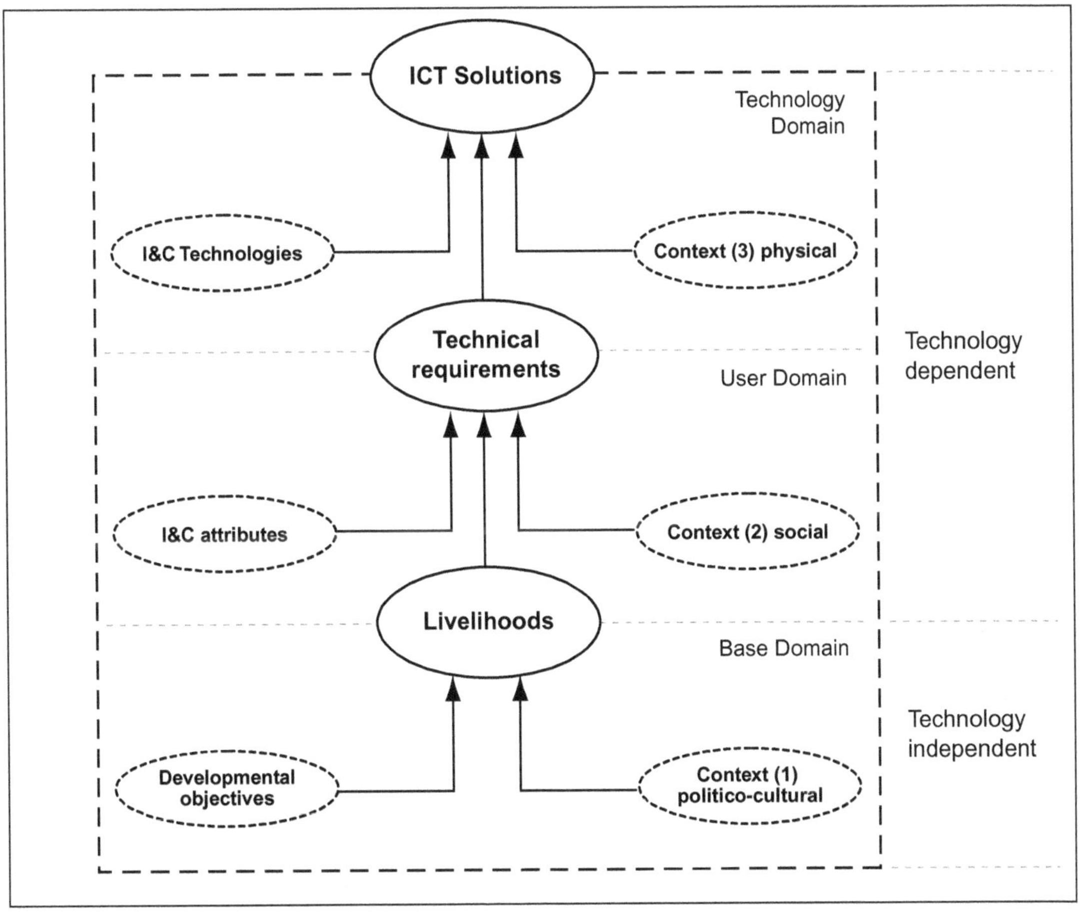

Each of the domains in the Percolator model is situated in the context of a predominant discipline: politico-cultural, social and physical. The domains interact through well defined interfaces across which solution baskets are passed. These baskets (livelihoods, technical requirements and ultimately, ICT solutions) represent distillations of requirements and considerations, drawn from the backdrop of various predominant disciplines. The baskets progressively constrain the ultimate solution as their refinements percolate up the model. The philosophical underpinnings of the model are reflected in this progressive "percolation" of solution features which ultimately constrain the choice of technological solutions.

While the User and Technology domains of the Percolator model are technology dependent, the Base Domain is technology independent. The livelihoods that derive from this domain form the basis of many solution "trees" which may be conceived using fundamentally different technologies.

1.1. AN EXAMPLE ICT SOLUTION TREE

As an example, an ICT solution tree may be built on a Base domain which favours trade as a key dimension of community livelihood. In this domain, the selection of trade is made on the basis of the political and cultural context of the community and on the basis that trade is an effective avenue to realize economic development as one important national objective.

In the User domain, an ICT solution tree defines the attributes ascribed to information and communications, for example quantity and quality of information and its flow characteristics. Information and communications attributes appropriate to the community are selected from among these on the basis of appropriate livelihoods, as defined in the Base domain, as well as on the basis of the social context of the community. For example the type of trade envisioned may require the communication of the equivalent of 6,000 words of locally-generated information between one central location and fifty homes twice each day. The social context may constrain the technical requirements of information and communications technologies to audio or visual formats rather than text-based formats, as would be the case for communities in which the levels of basic literacy are very low. Another of the many aspects of the social context is the profile of the community's existing communications uptake. For example, if the vast majority of households enjoy television, a technical requirement may be that the user interface is a television.

In the Technology domain, a variety of information and communications technologies are defined. Those whose user interface is a television include various technologies which use terrestrial microwave transmission as well as cable, LMDS and different satellite technologies. Many factors derived from the community's physical context strongly influence the selection from among these technologies. These include the penetration rates of televisions in homes; the installed base, and state of repair, of existing television distribution infrastructure; the terrain; the geographical extent of the community and the distribution of households within the community. Taking account of these physical considerations in the community of interest, as well as of the technical requirements articulated by the User domain, the ultimate ICT solution for this community may be Low Power Television (LPTV).

2. Contextualization in the Percolator Model

The Percolator model recognizes the tremendous significance of context in the ultimate selection of technologies to facilitate development. This is especially so for technologies which serve an *indirect* purpose, as is the case for ICT in pro-poor intervention. For these communities, the model borrows heavily from the UNDP Sustainable Livelihood Approach, SLA (Singh & Wanmali, 1998; Wanmali, 1998; Ashley & Carney; 1999) and DFID's Sustainable Livelihoods (SL), which are driven by an assessment of community strengths and assets rather than by an assessment of (perceived) needs.[2]

The many contextual parameters taken into account in SL include *"the priorities that people identify; the different strategies they adopt in pursuit of their priorities; the institutions, policies and organizations that determine their access to assets/opportunities and the returns they can achieve; their access to social, human, physical, financial and natural capital, and their ability to put these to productive use and the context in which they live, including external trends (economic, technological, demographic, etc.), shocks (natural or man-made), and seasonality"* (Ashley & Carney, 1999).

These context parameters, and many more, are fundamental to the proposition that ICT can effectively impact on *economic* poverty alleviation. Economic and enterprise parameters are less important to the alleviation of *digital* poverty but social parameters are equally important.

The Percolator model accounts for context parameters according to their domain/s of influence (Base, User and Technology) and to the extent to which the impact they exert is of primary or secondary importance. Parameters that exert stronger ("primary") influence are weighted more heavily than those that exert less ("secondary") influence.

---

[2] Guidance Sheets available at http://www.livelihoods.org/info/info_guidancesheets.html#7.

3. The Base Domain

Digitally impoverished communities differ in very many ways including their phys-ical extent, level of urbanization, culture, geography and demographics. SLA advances a comprehensive approach to determining sustainable livelihoods by tak-ing account of the macro-, micro and sectoral policies that impact on livelihood and the use of individual and collective assets as well as community strengths, con-straints, institutions and priorities to envision new and nominally-disruptive liveli-hoods. In the Base Domain of the Percolator model, features of appropriate liveli-hoods are developed through standard technology-independent SLA analysis. Case studies, included in the DFID Guidance Sheets and elsewhere (e.g. Singh & Wanmali, 1998; Ashley & Carney, 1999), describe how the analysis can be performed to establish general features of the many dimensions of sustainable livelihoods in a variety of different communities.

SLA provides the overarching framework for the Percolator model. The model adds fresh insights into the process of selecting information and communications technologies for sustainable livelihoods and therefore focuses much of its attention on the User and Technology Domains.

4. The User Domain

Objectives for ICT-based intervention may be categorized as secondary or as pri-mary. Secondary objectives comprise all developmental targets that may be achieved indirectly through the application of ICT, for example those relating to the Millennium Development Goals. These include health, education, environmental sustainability and enterprise. Secondary objectives are technology independent and are implicitly accounted for in the livelihoods that percolate up to the User domain from the Base domain.

Primary objectives are specified in terms of sectoral metrics which, for ICT-based pro-poor intervention relate directly to digital poverty. Barrantes' chapter in this book discusses the notion of digital poverty and analyses the demand side of ICT in digitally impoverished communities. This analysis, together with other realities such as the profile of basic literacy within a community, constitutes the social con-text for ICT-based intervention and is accounted for in the User Domain of the Percolator model.

4.1. ATTRIBUTES OF INFORMATION AND COMMUNICATIONS
The attributes of information and communications constitute the other major cate-gory of considerations in the User Domain of an ICT solution tree in the Percolator

model. These generic attributes are independent of the specific technologies used to deliver information and communications services. The decoupling of information and communications *attributes* from information and communications *technologies* is key to the Percolator model as it enables the ultimate selection of technologies on the basis of the features of information (useful to particular communities) and on the basis of suitable ways in which community members communicate this information.

The basic attributes ascribed to generic information are:

1. Its intrinsic format (e.g., audio, image, numeric, etc.)

2. The quantity of data required to represent it digitally.

As all forms of intrinsic information may be represented and communicated digitally, communications attributes have less to do with the intrinsic form of the information conveyed and more to do with its data equivalence and the needs of communicating parties. For example if two community members wish to communicate with each other through conversational voice while two others wish to communicate through voice messaging, the nature of the intrinsic information, audio, is unchanged while the *communications attributes* (synchronous in the first case and asynchronous in the second) are quite different.

As another example, members of a community may lack basic literacy and therefore not be able to interact through text-based information. For such a community, information may only be effectively communicated through video or audio means. In this case, the social context constrains the *communications attribute* to a particular medium (video or audio), independent of the native format of the information to be communicated.

Accordingly, Table 1 documents the range of attributes that may be ascribed to the *communication* of information and inherently incorporates the notion of the quantity of (digital) *information* to be communicated.

The table categorizes communications attributes according to whether or not the medium is constrained by social factors as well as to its rate, its flow, its symmetry, its topology and the extent to which mobility and ubiquity are required. The table includes attributes that relate to key social parameters of particular communities, for example where access points are located and users' requirements for familiarity with communications appliances as well as the value they place on the appliances' ease of use and flexibility.

Table 1: **Information and Communications Attributes with Qualitative Reference Points**

Communications Attributes	Reference Points		
	Low	**Mid-range**	**High**
Basic attributes			
i) Medium, if constrained	Constrained to audio (or unconstrained)	Text-based (or unconstrained)	Constrained to video (or unconstrained)
ii) Rate	Low	Moderate	High
iii) Flow	Interactive	Streaming	Conversational / real time
iv) Mobility	None (fixed)	Low mobility	High mobility
v) Symmetry	One-way only	One-way at a time	Two-way simultaneously
vi) Topology	Two particular communicators	One to many particular communicators	Arbitrary one to one communicators
vii) Ubiquity	Access only to local community	Access to local community and to other particular communities	Global access, access to the Internet and / or to the PSTN
viii) Location of access points	Single center	Multiple centers	Anywhere
Attributes of Appliance			
i) Familiarity	Very familiar	Moderately familiar	Not familiar at all
ii) Usability	Very easy to use	Manageable	Complicated
iii) Flexibility	Inflexible: supports single application	Somewhat flexible: supports limited range of applications	Very flexible: supports rich variety of applications

Information and communications attributes are important as the *social* basis for selecting technological solutions which are appropriate to, and adopted by, communities of interest. Their correspondence with physical, human, social and cultural factors is therefore very important as the latter figure strongly in the adoption, application, and use of new technologies in general and ICT in particular (e.g. Tse et al., 2004).

The attributes of Table 1 bare natural linkages to their application in a social setting. For example they describe the quantity and flow of information to be communicated using ICT, the relationships between communicating entities, the manner in which they interact, the extent to which they are on the move while they communicate and where they communicate from. The attributes also describe the ultimate (global) geographic reach of communications from the community and capture considerations relating to user needs with respect to the devices they use to communicate.

Table 2 provides a matrix of technical parameters that correspond to the attributes of Table 1. These parameters include format, data rate, delay, delay variation, frame error rate, transmission media, MAC protocol, transmission symmetry, logical and physical topology, internetworking, profile of uptake locally, regionally and globally, as well as the level of technological maturity and the simplicity and range of capabilities of the end user appliance.

Low, mid-range and high values for each parameter are provided in Table 2. Parameter values do not correlate down columns as the entries are independent of each other. In general, particular communications profiles are therefore described by some mix of low-range, mid-range and high-range parameters.

Table 2: **Technical Parameters Corresponding to Communications Attributes**

Communications Attribute	Corresponding Technical Parameter	Reference Points for Technical Parameter		
		Low	Mid-range	High
Basic attributes				
i) Medium, if constrained	Format	Audio	Text	Video
ii) Rate	Data rate	4 – 64 kbps	≈ 384 kbps	≥10 Mbps
iii) Flow	Delay	> 10 sec	> 150 ms; < 10 sec	< 150 ms
	Delay variation	N/A	N/A	< 1 ms
	Frame Error Rate	< 3%	< 1%	0%
iv) Mobility	Transmission Media	Wired or wireless	Wireless	Wireless
	MAC Protocol	N/A	Mobility management	Mobility management
v) Symmetry	Transmission symmetry	Simplex	Half duplex	Full duplex
vi) Topology	Logical topology	Point to point link	Broadcast network	Peer to peer network
vii) Ubiquity	Internetworking	Stand alone local network	Local net linked to specific other community nets	Local network with backhaul to the Internet and/or to PSTN
	Profile of local, regional and global uptake	One of: local, regional, global or minimal installed base	Two of: local, regional, global or only modest installed base	Widespread local, regional and global deployment
viii) Location of access points	Physical topology	Single link	Thin network	Dense network
Attributes of Appliance				
i) Familiarity	i) Maturity	Mature technology: familiar end user appliance and operation	Well established technology: familiar end user appliance but new operation or vice versa	New technology: unfamiliar end user appliance and operation
ii) Usability	ii) Simplicity	No installation or configuration required of user. Operation simple	Some installation and configuration required of user. Operation somewhat simple	Complicated installation, configuration & operation
iii) Flexibility	iii) Range	Supports only basic communications	Supports entertainment and access to services	Supports a wide range of applications including revenue generating ones

This table only represents the technical parameters that correspond to communications attributes which are of direct significance to users. It does not represent the many derivative technical parameters such as channel bandwidth whose requirements are derived from a combination of the required data rate, coding, modulation scheme and Bit Error Rate.

Tables 3 and 4 provide an example which illustrates the manner in which the attributes of information and communications appropriate to a particular social context maps onto technical parameters.

In the example in Tables 3 and 4, low data rate, one way communications conveying streaming (voice) information between arbitrary communicators anywhere in a local community using a familiar user interface without support for mobility is satisfied by the provision of simplex communications over a wired or wireless peer to peer network with the following technical requirements: a data rate of 4 kbps, a delay variation of less than 1 ms, a frame error rate of less than 3% and little constraint on absolute delay.

The generic technical requirements that emerge from the User domain 'percolate up' to the Technology domain where specific ICT solutions are derived, taking

Table 3: **Example Profile of ICT Attributes**

Communications	Reference Points		
Attributes	**Low**	**Mid-range**	**High**
Basic attributes			
i) Medium, if constrained	**Constrained to audio (or unconstrained)**	Text-based (or unconstrained)	Constrained to video (or unconstrained)
ii) Rate	**Low**	Moderate	High
iii) Flow	Interactive	**Streaming**	Conversational / real time
iv) Mobility	**None (fixed)**	Low mobility	High mobility
v) Symmetry	**One-way only**	One-way at a time	Two-way simultaneously
vi) Topology	Two particular communicators	One to many particular communicators	**Arbitrary one to one communicators**
vii) Ubiquity	**Access only to local community**	Access to local community and to other particular communities	Global access, access to the Internet and / or to the PSTN
viii) Access points	Single center	Multiple centers	**Anywhere**
Attributes of Appliance			
i) Familiarity	**Very familiar**	Moderately familiar	Not familiar at all
ii) Usability	Very easy to use	**Manageable**	Complicated
iii) Flexibility	Inflexible: supports single application	**Somewhat flexible: supports limited range of applications**	Very flexible: supports rich variety of applications

additional account of physical contextualization and the available range of ICT. In the example illustrated by Tables 3 and 4, voice messaging over the PSTN would be strongly suggested if the community enjoys a comprehensive PSTN installed base.

Table 4: **Technical Parameters (Linked to Corresponding Service Attributes) with Reference Points for Technical Requirements**

Communications Attribute	Corresponding Technical Parameter	Reference Points for Technical Parameter		
		Low	Mid-range	High
Basic attributes				
i) Medium, if constrained	Format	**Audio**	Text	Video
ii) Rate	Data rate	**4 – 64 kbps**	≈ 384 kbps	≥10 Mbps
iii) Flow	Delay	**> 10 sec**	> 150 ms; < 10 sec	< 150 ms
	Delay variation	N/A	N/A	< 1 ms
	Frame Error Rate	**< 3%**	**< 1%**	0%
iv) Mobility	Transmission Media	**Wired or wireless**	Wireless	Wireless
	MAC Protocol	**N/A**	Mobility management	Mobility management
v) Symmetry	Transmission symmetry	**Simplex**	Half duplex	Full duplex
vi) Topology	Logical topology	Point to point link	Broadcast network	**Peer to peer network**
vii) Ubiquity	Internetworking	**Stand alone local network**	Local net linked to specific other community nets	Local network with backhaul to the Internet and/or to PSTN
	Profile of local, regional and global uptake	One of: local, regional, global or minimal installed base	Two of: local, regional, global or only modest installed base	Widespread local, regional and global deployment
viii) Location of access points	Physical topology	Single link	Thin network	**Dense network**
Attributes of User Interface				
i) Familiarity	i) Maturity	**Mature technology: familiar end user appliance and operation**	Well established technology: familiar end user appliance but new operation or vice versa	New technology: unfamiliar end user appliance and operation
ii) Usability	ii) Simplicity	No installation or configuration required of user. Operation simple	**Some installation and configuration required of user. Operation somewhat simple**	Complicated installation, configuration & operation
iii) Flexibility	iii) Range	Supports only basic communications	**Supports entertainment and access to services**	Supports a wide range of applications including revenue generating ones

5. The Technology Domain

The Technology Domain defines the range of available technologies, their corresponding technical characteristics and the manner in which physical considerations constrain their use. These technologies are evaluated against the technical requirements established by the User Domain in order to propose contextually appropriate information and communications technologies.

Key categories of ICT of relevance to pro-poor intervention are access technologies, access device technologies and application technologies. The first play a central role in the penetration of ICT into digitally poor communities while the second and third figure strongly in the level of uptake by community members.

5.1. ACCESS TECHNOLOGIES

Access technologies are those that enable communication between end users and core networks. They are the conduit, as it were, for the delivery of communications services from service providers directly to end users. Technologies traditionally used for this purpose include telephony, television and radio, the latter including amateur and other forms of push to talk technologies. Not withstanding the fact that data communications has proliferated over the past few decades, these traditional access technologies and their modern variants, such as digital TV, are important propositions for intervention.

At the other end of the spectrum lie fiber optic access technologies. Their high bandwidth, combined with superlative quality, make these the technologies of choice, where available, for fixed users with flexible budgets and sophisticated application requirements. The substantial infrastructural and deployment costs, low architectural reconfigurability and flexibility as well as limited deployment, make them unattractive for traditionally poor communities in developing countries.

The many wired broadband access technologies which utilize traditional infrastructure at relatively low marginal cost offer significant potential for communities in which the infrastructure exists. Such technologies include Broadband over PowerLine (BPL), which uses the ubiquitous installed base of power distribution companies, as well as Cable access and xDSL which leverage existing Cable TV and POTS infrastructure respectively.

Wireless access technologies have attracted a great deal of attention for unconnected communities (see for example Jhunjhunwala & Orne, 2003). The most compelling advantages of these technologies are the ease, speed and low cost of deployment which can enable rapid and widespread ICT diffusion. Within the smorgasbord of wireless access possibilities, cellular networks offer mobility as well as particularly wide coverage. Like cellular wireless technologies, satellite-based access technologies offer wide coverage but variously with and without mobility. Many offer the additional benefit of swift installation and, for this reason, are particularly useful in disaster recovery and other applications which require rapid deployment of temporary communications services. While cellular and satellite technologies generally feature wide coverage, wireless LAN (WLAN) technologies such as WiFi, WiMAX and Mobile-Fi deliver particularly high data rates at limited mobility and some broadband wireless access technologies, such as MMDS and LMDS, represent fixed wireless solutions.

Much has been documented on the technical features of various access technologies. Comparisons between access technologies are also widely available in the literature, for example WiFi has been compared to 3G cellular (Lehr & McKnight, 2003), to Bluetooth (Ferro & Potorti, 2005), to WiMax (Otero, 2004) and to other 3G alternatives (Alvén et al., 2001).

5.2. ACCESS DEVICE TECHNOLOGIES

Communications appliances, often referred to as "access devices", represent the interface through which users access information and communications services. They are of considerable significance within the Percolator Model as they are associated with various context parameters such as affordability, availability, simplicity, interactivity, mobility, ubiquity, accessibility, computational power, power requirements, portability, user friendliness and environmental operating features. These context parameters are accounted for partly in the User domain and partly in the Technology domain.

Devices traditionally used to access communications services include the land line telephone, the television and various forms of radio. Many digitally poor communities have long traditions of radio and television access. Especially for communities in which basic literacy rates are very low, these appliances figure strongly in the selection of access device technology and correspondingly to access technologies themselves. A rich array of television and broadcast radio technologies exist, many of which feature transition paths to digital literacy. Set top boxes, for example, may be used with traditional television appliances and keyboards to access the Internet.

Other access devices include mobile phones, desktop PCs, handhelds and even the Simple Inexpensive Multilingual People's Computer, Simputer, the VolksComputer (Riti, 2001; Vaughan, 2005) and the VillagePDA (Wattegama, 2004). Many of these cater for the special needs of various communities by, for example, making use of touch screens for users who lack basic literacy skills and by featuring interfaces in local languages.

5.3. APPLICATION TECHNOLOGIES

Application technologies refer to the end user capabilities possible through information and communications technologies. These capabilities, "applications", refer to software programs which run on access devices in order to provide value added capabilities on top of basic communications services or to the capabilities enabled directly through basic communications services. Examples of the former are email clients and Web browsers which run on access devices and through which email and Web browsing services are possible, respectively. An example of the latter is television, which is accessible directly from the access device.

The proposition of ICT-based intervention is intimately tied to end user applications. This association is built into each layer in the Percolator model, with the strongest influence accounted for in the Base domain which defines the general scope of activities that ICT applications facilitate, for example farming, trade, industry, health, education, commerce etc. Applications consistent with this general scope and satisfying the technical requirements articulated in the User domain, are selected in the Technology domain taking additional account of many aspects of the physical context of the community.

5.4. PHYSICAL CONTEXT

The Base and User Domains of the Percolator Model take into consideration various human and social context parameters that collectively constrain the choice of ICT for sustainable development in communities under threat of digital exclusion. The Technology Domain refines the range of suitable ICT, not only on the basis of the range of available technologies and their technical requirements for particular communities, as percolated up from the Base and User domains, but also on the basis of the physical context which characterizes particular application environments.

The physical parameters that impact on the choice of ICT for pro-poor intervention are widely varied and include environmental and topographical profiles of communities, many dimensions of the physical wherewithal of community members as well as the physical availability of human resource, infrastructural and ancillary support required to deploy, maintain and access information and communications services.

Physical parameters impact on the choice of ICT in many ways. For example, the geographical extent of a community, its remoteness, localized population settlement, growth and migration patterns constrain the network architecture, physical topology, scale, scalability and internetworking requirements of appropriate local networks and their wide area counterparts. The topographical profile of the land, the nature of the natural and man-made structures, climactic conditions and natural vulnerabilities as well as the profile of spurious electromagnetic radiation and vulnerabilities to physical intrusion and vandalism are key considerations in the choice of transmission media and various other transmission parameters, including transmission frequencies in the case of wireless access.

The maturity of technology standards, the degree to which technologies under consideration comply with international standards, the literature available on the technologies and their uptake locally, regionally and globally are important considerations as they impact on the ultimate ubiquity of communications as well as on the availability and cost of equipment and spares. The existence of legacy communications infrastructure and ancillary services, such as electricity supply and transportation are also important factors in the contemplation of network implementation and ultimately on the price of service to community members. Additionally, the level of regulatory barriers to network deployment and operation are key considerations.

The wherewithal of community members to access ICT through subscription rates, language, literacy, vision, hearing and other means or at various locations are also significant determinants of appropriate technologies.

Table 5 provides an example of the manner in which the technical parameters of technologies may be compared in accordance with the frameworks of Tables 1 and 2, taking account of the physical context of particular communities as described above. It presents these parameters according to thematic classifications: standards, network architecture, transmission, interface, deployment, application support and 'other'. For simplicity, the table charts an inexhaustive set of access technologies. It does not include the full range of information and communications technologies, as have been briefly discussed in this section.

Table 5 provides a framework, rather than a blueprint, for the categorization of technologies according to technical parameters which derive from the information and communications attributes that are appropriate to particular communities. These attributes are selected on the basis of contextualization in the three domains of the Percolator model, as described in the current and previous sections of this chapter.

In many cases single technologies straddle two or even three reference ranges in the table because it provides coarse characterizations without regard for the many subtleties of technological capabilities. Implementation of the Percolator model accounts for this fuzziness by recognizing the operational conditions of each technology that may place it in each of the possible reference ranges. For example, in infrastructure mode WiFi networks are implemented with point to point network architectures while in ad hoc mode they are implemented using point to multipoint architectures. Also, their nominal coverage range is 500 ft indoors and 1000 ft outdoors, but they may be specially equipped for extended coverage. As another example, WiFi implementations trade off performance against spectral efficiency, depending on which parameter is more highly valued. Therefore one implementation of a technology may fall into one range in the table while another implementation of the same technology may fall into another.

Table 5: **Sample Mappings of Access Technologies to Reference Technical Parameter Ranges**

Technical Parameter	Reference Points		
	Low	**Mid-range**	**High**
Standards:			
Uptake	One of: local, regional, global or minimal installed base • 3G, FTTH, WiMax, BPL	Two of: local, regional, global or only modest installed base • LMDS/MMDS	Widespread local, regional and global deployment • POTS, WiFi, xDSL, VSAT
Compliance and Maturity	Emerging • WiMax, BPL	New or maturing • 3G, WLL, WiFi, FTTH	Mature • POTS, xDSL, VSAT, LMDS, MMDS, Cellular, CATV
Network architecture:			
Scalability of protocol suite	Protocol suite not scalable by service • POTS, xDSL, VSAT, CATV	Protocol moderately scalable by service • LMDS, MMDS,WLL, WiFi, WiMax, FTTH, BPL	Protocol suite highly scalable by service • 3G, WiMax
Topology	Point to point link • LMDS, WiMAX, VSAT, leased line	One to many network • CATV, BPL, WiMax MMDS,WLL, VSAT, POTS, xDSL, FTTH	Many to many (i.e. mesh or partial mesh) network • WiFi, POTS, xDSL, FTTH, WLL, LMDS, 3G
Physical architecture	Highly structured architecture • POTS, xDSL, FTTH, CATV, BPL	Lightly structured architecture • 3G, VSAT, LMDS/MMDS, WLL, WiMax	Ad hoc architecture • WiFi
Reconfigurability	Difficult to reconfigure • 3G, POTS, xDSL, FTTH, CATV, BPL	Moderately easy to reconfigure • VSAT, LMDS/MMDS	Easily reconfigured • WiFi, WLL, WiMax
WAN architecture	No cost: local network only, no backhaul • WiFi	Moderate cost: e.g. service provider leases backhaul services • WLL, WiMax	High cost: e.g. service provider implements and maintains backhaul • LMDS, MMDS, VSAT, 3G, POTS, xDSL, BPL
Local network architecture	No media to install • 3G, WiFi, WiMax, VSAT	Hybrid media: some cabling to install • WLL, LMDS, MMDS, xDSL	Wired media to install • POTS, CATV, FTTH, BPL
Network design	Minimal technical expertise required to design and scale network • WiFi	Moderate technical expertise required to design and scale network • WiMax, VSAT, WLL	Advanced technical expertise required to design and scale network • 3G, LMDS/MMDS, POTS, FTTH, CATV, BPL, xDSL
Internetworking	Stand alone local network • WiFi	Local network linked to specific other community networks • WiMax	Local network with backhaul to the Internet and / or to PSTN • POTS, xDSL, 3G, VSAT, WLL, LMDS/MMDS, FTTH, CATV, BPL
Scalability requirements	No economies of scale • VSAT	Moderate economies of scale • POTS, xDSL, WiFi	Significant economies of scale • 3G, WiMax
Physical security	Medium and terminal equipment very vulnerable to shocks and intrusion • POTS, xDSL, BPL	Medium and terminal equipment moderately vulnerable to shocks and intrusion • 3G, VSAT, WLL, LMDS/MMDS	Medium equipment robust against shocks and terminal equipment minimally vulnerable to shocks and intrusion • FTTH, CATV, WiFi, WiMax
Literature available	Comprehensive technical and commercialization information readily available • 3G, VSAT, POTS, xDSL	Some technical and commercialization information available • LMDS/MMDS, FTTH, CATV	Comprehensive technical and commercialization information not available • WiFi, WiMax, BPL
Cost to install and operate user equipment	None • Only special cases	Moderate • WiFi, WiMax, 3G, POTS, xDSL, BPL	High • VSAT, LMDS/MMDS, FTTH, CATV

Service cost	None • WiFi (some cases)	Moderate • 3G, POTS, xDSL, BPL	High • VSAT, LMDS/MMDS, FTTH, CATV, 3G
Transmission:			
Bandwidth	64 kbps • POTS, VSAT	512 kbps – 10 Mbps • xDSL, CATV, WiFi, VSAT, WLL, 3G	$\geq$ 10 Mbps • BPL, FTTH, WiFi, WiMax, LMDS/MMDS
BER	10^{-3} • 3G, WiFi	10^{-6} • POTS, xDSL	$\leq 10^{-9}$ • FTTH, CATV
Timing	Unbuffered asynchronous • WiFi	Buffered asynchronous • POTS, xDSL, BPL, VSAT	Buffered asynchronous or synchronous • FTTH, CATV, 3G, POTS
Encryption	No encryption	Light encryption • WiFi, WiMax, BPL	Robust encryption • VSAT, 3G, FTTH, CATV, xDSL
Mode	Simplex • Traditional CATV, radio broadcast	Half duplex • Push to talk radio, Amateur radio	Full duplex • 3G, WLL, xDSL, POTS, BPL, WiFi, WiMax, VSAT, FTTH, LMDS/MMDS
Delay	Days Mechanical technologies (e.g. "SneakerNet")	100s of microseconds VSAT, XDSL, WiFi, WiMax	Imperceptible 3G, LMDS/MMDS, FTTH, CATV, POTS
Max geographic range	300 m • WiFi	3 km • POTS, LMDS, CATV, FTTH, xDSL	$\geq$ 30 km • MMDS, WLL, WiMax, 3G, VSAT
Media	Wired • CATV, FTTH, xDSL,	Wireless MAN • WiFi, WiMax, MDS/MMDS, WLL, VSAT	Cellular • 3G
Signal propagation and penetrability characteristics	Wired media: robust signal • CATV, FTTH, xDSL, POTS, BPL	Low frequency wireless transmission: moderately sensitive to environmental conditions and mediocre penetrability • 3G, WiFi, WiMax	High frequency wireless transmission: sensitive to environmental conditions and poor penetrability • LMDS/MMDS, WLL, VSAT
Media subject to regulatory costs	Transmission disallowed • Some wireless frequencies and cable paths in some jurisdictions	Transmission allowed with modest barriers • 3G, CATV, xDSL, BPL	Transmission allowed with few or no barriers • WiMax, WiFi
Media subject to regulatory costs	No costs for right of way or licenses • WiFi (typically)	Low costs of one or both: right of way and licenses • CATV, FTTH, xDSL, POTS, BPL	High costs for right of way and licenses • 3G, WiMax, LMDS/MMDS, WLL, VSAT
Interface:			
Accessibility to differently-abled users	Standard interfaces alone • xDSL, POTS	Subset of interfaces with voice activation, touch screen, audio output • CATV	Interfaces with voice activation, touch screen, audio output • FTTH, 3G, WiFi, WiMax, LMDS/MMDS, WLL, VSAT
Accessibility to diverse language groups	Interface presented in single language	Interface presented in more than one international language	Interface presented in international language as well as dialects
Familiarity	Unfamiliar end user appliance and operation • WiFi, WiMax, LMDS/MMDS, VSAT, FTTH	Familiar end user appliance but new operation or vice versa • xDSL, BPL, CATV, WLL	Familiar end user appliance and operation • POTS, 3G
Usability	Complicated installation, configuration & operation • LMDS/MMDS, VSAT, FTTH	Some installation and configuration required of user. Operation somewhat simple • WiFi, WiMax, xDSL, BPL, CATV, WLL	No installation or configuration required of user. Operation simple • POTS, 3G
Deployment:			
Time to deploy	Days • VSAT, WiFi,	Months • WiMax, xDSL, 3G	Years • CATV, LMDS/MMDS, FTTH

In the Technology domain the relative weightings attached to physical resources, including available spectrum and maximum transmit power restrictions, are taken into account in the selection of base technologies and their particular implementations.

5.5. ICT SOLUTIONS

The ultimate ICT solutions that are selected at the top of the Percolator model enable end user applications which are in turn enabled by information and communications services, whose technical requirements are well documented.

As is the case for the Base Domain, the Technology Domain forms the basis of many solution "trees". In particular, each unique application environment can be associated with its own solution set comprising unique solution branches. The solution branches in turn comprise various combinations of technologies, appropriately adapted to the environment to provide individual solutions. It is these solutions, and not information and communication technologies of themselves, that represent tangible avenues for developmental impact. They variously surround applications relating to commerce, health, education, civic participation, news, cultural and artistic expression, entertainment, enterprise and a rich array of livelihoods.

For each solution tree, the Percolator model is implemented by using a custom weighting system attached to context parameters in each domain. For example, in the Technology domain, a community that lies at the heart of a hurricane belt will attach a particularly high weighting to natural disasters and consequently value physical security very highly. In communities whose buildings are constructed according to rigorous building codes, path obstruction is a particular concern and consequently wired technology solutions may be favored over their less robust wireless counterparts.

For poor communities, key parameters in the determination of ultimate ICT solutions often relate to the simplicity with which network infrastructure can be assembled and operated; the degree to which the network may grow and shrink in an ad hoc manner, the flexibility and accessibility of communications appliances and the energy requirements of network and user equipment. For such communities, the flexibility of multihop or mesh network architectures in ad hoc wireless networks (Corson & Macker, 1999) and the innovative use of supportive technologies including alternative energy technologies and open source software (Proenza, 2005) hold great potential, though there is much debate as to the total cost of ownership for the latter (UNCTAD, 2003; Dravis, 2004).

Quite apart from the choice of information and communications technologies, the success of ICT solutions for digitally poor communities is very closely linked to models of ownership as well as to service and access models. Galperin and Girard's chapter explore these dimensions.

Information and communications solutions span the range of technologies which are purely physical, such as Sneakernet, to the intermediate DakNet (Jhunjhunwal & Orne, 2003), to the purely digital. Financial, cultural and social constraints of low resource communities may well dictate a valid choice of non-technical or low-technical solutions notwithstanding the fact that this chapter has only considered purely digital solutions.

6. Conclusion

In the Percolator model, the ultimate application for which ICTs are used is tied closely to developmental objectives. The model offers a framework in which solutions may be contemplated in a systematic and manageable way, taking account of ultimate developmental objectives as well as various contextual parameters and the technical features of available information and communications technologies.

As with all frameworks, application of the Percolator model requires customization. In particular, the unique nature of various communities must be coded in a weighting scheme that applies to the many context parameters that have been partitioned according to three fundamental domains: Base, User and Technology. Ultimate ICT solutions, built on basic technologies, are tremendously influenced by innovative spins that derive from sensitivity to physical, social and politico-cultural contexts, a sensitivity that is refined through the systematic process of percolation. Solutions range from generic use of standard technologies and application philosophies to the use of many technologies in hybrid solutions.

This chapter has focused on ICT solution trees in the Percolator model. Nevertheless, the model is far more general and may be applied to a number of other technologies. For example, a Base domain which favors livelihoods that incorporate some element of trade, as an economic agent and based on strong cultural traditions, may form the basis of a solution tree constructed for mechanical technologies. In the User domain, such a tree incorporates the attributes ascribed to transport for example: speed, waiting time, number of passengers, space for goods, seating arrangement, cleanliness, regularity. The attributes, filtered by the social context, determine the technical requirements of transportation technologies appropriate to community members. These requirements constitute the technical requirements basket and are specified as far as possible in quantitative terms, for example "a minimum speed of 2 miles per hour" or "a minimum capacity of two human beings and 5 cubic feet of storage space". The technical requirements basket forms the basis of the choice of transportational technologies among those that are possible for the community (for example donkey cart, private car and public bus) and motivate particular choices (for example donkey cart) of transport to best serve the purposes of particular community members. The Percolator model may therefore be applied to intervention based on a variety of different technological disciplines.

The model provides an incremental approach to solution deployment and implementation, particularly well suited to communities of severely limited resources. It describes an iterative process of solution finding that tracks the dynamism of developmental targets and available technologies.

At the heart of the Percolator model is the separation of the attributes of information and communications from the technologies used to deliver information and communications services. This, along with the model's deep emphasis on the many dimensions of contextualization, is important in ensuring that ICT are introduced in a manner that is acceptable and accessible to community members. This, in turn, is vital to the gradual but effective adoption of ICT by communities that are under serious threat of digital exclusion.

References

Alvén, D., Arjunanpillai, R., Farhang, R., Kansal, S., Khan, N. & Leufven, U. (2001). Hotspots – Connect the Dots for a Wireless Future. *Final report on Analysis of a 3G alternative for Ericsson Business Innovation and Telia Research.* Retrieved from http://www.dsv.su.se/~mab/Alven.pdf.

Ashley, C. & Carney, D. (1999). *Sustainable Livelihoods: Lessons from early experience.* London: DFID.

Avgerou, C. (2000). Recognizing Alternative Rationalities in the Deployment of Information Systems. *The Electronic Journal on Information Systems in Developing Countries, 3*(7), 1-15.

Cecchini S. & Shah T. (2002). *Information and Communications Technology as a Tool for Empowerment. World Bank Empowerment Sourcebook: Tools and Practices 1.* Washington, DC: The World Bank.

Corson, S. & Macker, J. (1999). *Mobile Ad-hoc Networking (MANET).* IETF RFC 2501, January. Retrieved from http://www.faqs.org/rfcs/rfc2501.html

Davis, F.D. (1993). User Acceptance of Information Technology: System characteristics, user perceptions and behavioral impacts. *International Journal of Man-Machine Studies, Vol. 38*, pp. 475-87.

DFID. (2002). The Significance of Information and Communication Technologies for Reducing Poverty. London: DFID. Retrieved September, 2005, from http://www.dfid.gov.uk/pubs/files/ictpoverty.pdf

Dravis, P. (2003). Open Source Software: Perspectives for Development. World Bank (InfoDev). Retrieved July, 2005, from http://wbln0018.worldbank.org/ict/resources.nsf/D045B0DD4551DA0885256B29005FCE67/879F7A7745A5053D85256E750063416D?OpenDocument.

Ferro, E. & Potorti, F. (2005). *Bluetooth and Wi-Fi Wireless Protocols: A survey and comparison.* IEEE Wireless Communications. Retrieved from http://dienst.isti.cnr.it/Dienst/Repository/2.0/Body/ercim.cnr.isti/2004-TR-27/pdf?tiposearch=cnr&langver=

G-8. (2000). *Okinawa Charter on the Global Information Society.* G8 Information Centre. Toronto: University of Toronto.

Jhunjhunwala, N. & Orne, P. (2003). *The Wireless Internet Opportunity for Developing Countries.* The Wireless Internet Institute (Ed.). Washington, D.C.: World Times, Inc. InfoDev.

Lehr, W. & McKnight, L. (2003). Wireless Internet access: 3G vs. WiFi? *Telecommunications Policy, 27*, 351–370.

Otero, J. (2004). WiFi and WiMax. *Caribbean Telecoms Briefing, Part 1.* London: Informa Telecoms Group.

Proenza, F. (2005). Strategic Open Source Software: Choice for Developing Country Governments. *i4d magazine June 2005.* Retrieved September, 2005, from http://www.i4donline.net/june05/open-source.asp

Riti, M.D. (2001). *Simputer: The Computer for the Masses.* Rediff Business. Retrieved September, 2005, from http://www.rediff.com/money/2001/apr/24spec.htm

Tse, T., Tiong, J. & Kangaslahti, V. (2004). The Effect of Cultural Norms on the Uptake of Information and Communication Technologies in Europe: A Conceptual Analysis. *International Journal of Management*, 21(3) 382-392.

UNCTAD. (2003). E-Commerce and Development Report. UNCTAD/SDTE/ECB/2003/1. Retrieved July, 2005, from http://r0.unctad.org/ecommerce/ecommerce_en/edr03_en.htm

UNDP. (1996). *Human Development Report 1996.* New York: Oxford University Press. Retrieved June, 2005, from http://hdr.undp.org/reports/global/1996/en/

UNDP. (1999). New Technologies and the Global Race for Knowledge in Making New Technologies Work for Human Development. In UNDP *Human Development Report 1999*. New York: UNDP.

Vaughan, D. (2005). *ICT4D: An Integrated Approach for Village Communities*. Gladesville: Partners in Micro-Development.

Wanmali, S. (1998). Participatory Assessment and Planning for Sustainable Livelihoods. Retrieved August, from http://www.undp.org/sl/Documents/Strategy_papers/Participatory_Assessment_for_SLSW.htm/PAPSL.htm.

Wattegama, C. (2004). *Bridging the 'Analogue' and Digital Divides: The Unique Experience of Sri Lanka*. Second i4d Seminar, 27 – 28 August 2004. China. Retrieved September, 2005, from http://www.i4donline.net/events/2ndi4d/chanuka1.htm.

World Bank. (1999). *Knowledge for Development, World Development Report 1998/99*. Washington DC: World Bank. Retrieved September 20, 2005, from http://info.worldbank.org/ict/assets/docs/ExecSum.pdf

CHAPTER 7

Conclusion:
ICT and Pro-poor Strategies and Research

Amy Mahan
LIRNE.NET & COMUNICA

Abstract

This chapter amalgamates the different themes raised in this first collaborative initiative of the Regional Dialogue on the Information Society (REDIS-DIRSI). The research undertaken by the network addresses ICT demand and supply side issues, regulatory reform and the private sector, consumer advocacy, new ownership models for network service provision and emerging network technology solutions – especially from a pro-poor perspective. Accordingly, this concluding chapter traverses the different thematic areas, fitting them together both in terms of how they inform and feed into each other, and in the context of assessing the Latin American and Caribbean ICT terrain from a REDIS-DIRSI perspective.

The chapters in this book comprise the first collaborative initiative of the Regional Dialogue on the Information Society (REDIS-DIRSI), a Latin American and Caribbean research network committed to investigation, analysis, and developing pro-poor strategies for extending access to ICT resources within the region. Compounding the overarching fact of disparate levels of ICT access across countries and regions, clearly there are also policy and regulatory divergences, with vast apparent differences between nations' abilities to devise appropriate and effective information society policies, regulators' institutional capabilities and experience, and national legal frameworks, democratic traditions, and social infrastructure – all of which have bearing on future ability to participate in the information society and economy. Despite variance in the national level foundations for transcending weak ICT sectors, three things remain relatively constant:

1) The emerging "information society" and "information economy" give the telecom sector an exaggerated importance in determining the shape of modern economies and societies. A key element for devising effective policies is accurate and detailed assessments of the current ICT terrain.

2) Regulation is increasingly complex. Some of the primary contributors to this complexity include the changing nature of the companies being regulated (privatized, foreign-owned, multi-industry players), and the impact of new and converging technologies. For Latin America, the encroaching re-concentration of the telecom sector is of particular importance.

3) Policy and regulation play important roles in shaping the roll-out, affordability, quality, etc., of information infrastructures and of balancing the many competing interests concerned with such a central infrastructure. Protection of the consumer and universal service are particular challenges for LA&C.

This Conclusion surveys the issues raised in the preceding chapters. The overarching framework for the different analyses has been to grapple with identifying the necessary conditions to continue (or indeed put back on track) the impetus of regulatory reform and to extend ICT network sector growth for the LA&C region. In addition to strategies for affordable access, much of the work here is preoccupied with accurate assessments and accurate definitions of information and digital poverty, rather than relying on more generalized notions such as the "digital divide". New methodologies and indicators are viewed as essential starting points for creating policy to stimulate pro-poor adoption of ICT and effective and innovative uses of network infrastructure.

1. Indicators and Measuring Demand

In the good old days of POTs (plain old telephone service), teledensity was the essential indicator for taking the pulse of a country's infrastructure roll-out. A few other key indicators (such as mainlines per employees, faults per mainline, waiting lists, etc.) documented the efficiency and robustness of service provision.

With evolving infrastructure there is an urgency to develop new indicators to better assess progress and to identify both gaps and readiness for information society needs.[1] The Economist Intelligence Unit (EIU), for example, has just released its yearly e-readiness ranking for 2005. "A country's e-readiness is essentially a measure of its e-business environment, a collection of factors that indicate how amenable a market is to Internet-based opportunities."[2] There has been much effort in regulatory and ICT literature to correlate telecom infrastructure and economic growth. Not surprisingly, the methodology and ranking for the EIU study corresponds to evidence sought to demonstrate healthy regulatory environments and corresponding attention to universal service and access programs.

Of the LA&C countries forming part of the 65 countries surveyed, Table 1 shows their ranking in the EIU e-readiness study.[3]

Table 1: **EIU e-Readiness Ranking**

Country	Rank (out of 65)
Chile	31
Mexico	36
Brazil	38
Argentina	39
Jamaica	41
Venezuela	45
Colombia	48
Peru	50
Ecuador	55

Source: Economist Intelligence Unit (2005).

---

[1] For more detail on new indicators and measuring digital poverty, see also Minges (2005).

[2] EIU (2005).

[3] The EIU categories thus comprise: connectivity and technology infrastructure 25%; business environment 20%; consumer and business adoption 20%; legal and policy environment 15%; social and cultural environment 15%; and supporting e-services 5%. The EIU methodology weights infrastructure roll-out the highest – with the category criteria encompassing penetration of narrowband, broadband, mobile phone, Internet, PC, WiFi hotspots, Internet affordability, and security of Internet infrastructure.

The EIU ranking – and other methodologies – make it clear that economic development opportunities for countries become exponentially better as their score increases. Simply put, countries that have already achieved a high level of infrastructure roll-out have the luxury of allocating ICT spending on enhanced usage of ICT, rather than being bogged down in the intricacies of network roll-out and basic access. Or in other words, "[I]t is not simply that people in high-income countries have hundreds of times as many radios, televisions, phones, and other appliances than their counterparts in low-income countries. As the demands for the basic devices and services are satiated, other demands start to be filled. Countries begin to develop ICT-intensive industries and to intensify the ICT inputs to other, more traditional industries."[4]

Roxana Barrantes in her chapter (chapter 2) argues in the same vein, that those who are excluded from the network risk devolving into a vicious cycle of not having sufficient information about new technologies and services to engender demand based on perceived benefits. The definition of e-readiness is thus problematic – or inadequate in its assessment of levels of economic development for advanced e-commerce and e-services. At the other end of the spectrum, ICT for development and digital divide agendas have been preoccupied with affordability and access to a basic bundle of goods and services.

Barrantes emphasizes the importance of differentiating between *digital poverty* and *digital divides*. The latter concept has been the focus of much hype and generalization – typically summarized in terms such as ICT *haves and have nots*. Conversely, the notion of digital poverty attempts to define and measure the minimum levels of entry into ICT markets – the conditions required to create a basic level of informed demand. Thus, digital poverty can affect any segment of the population (not only the poor), and can be the result of different factors including economic poverty, supply-side failures, and insufficient information regarding benefits. By way of example, in her study aimed at better informing Peruvian information society policies, one-third of Peruvian households fell into the category of *extreme digital poverty*, compared with 18% of households identified as subject to *extreme economic poverty*.

Thus, there can be no single prescription for solutions to achieve universal service, simply because there are different reasons for the failure of the network to reach all potential consumers of telecom services. Gover Barja and Björn-Sören Gigler (chapter 1) further this discussion and proposes a methodology for measuring *information poverty* (in contrast to digital poverty) based on assessing the differ-

---

[4] See Daly (2004).

ences between localities within countries – rather than between countries – with this methodology comprising factors that underlie both supply and demand side limitations.

In a post-privatization context, market actors may not choose to service areas that are perceived as unprofitable – these include rural areas where it is costly to extend physical infrastructure and where lower population densities imply reduced demand and hence reduced revenues. It is often claimed that failure to extend the network occurs due to market factors such as lack of economies of scale in extending the network and offering service. However, it is increasingly found that poor and marginalized communities are willing to spend proportionately higher amounts on telecom services than in places with developed infrastructure. It has also been demonstrated that viable markets exist where network operators fear to tread. Thus, we need better models for assessing whether unmet universal service objectives constitute sites of market failure, or poor regulatory environments. Barja and Gigler's methodology attempts to capture these elements at a local level, and further to quantify the cost of equal access across communities in a particular country.

By way of example, a key difference between developed and developing country ICT environments is access outside of key cities. Rural access problems do persist for already developed economies, but tend to manifest at the level of broadband access to Internet services rather than a paucity of any ICT resources at all. Hence, universal access programs for developing countries will have a very different focus than those in countries with more mature infrastructure. "Almost half (46%) of LA&C lives at population densities below 150 (a conventional threshold for urban areas), and more than 90% of this group is at least an hour distant from a city; about a third of them (18% of LA&C total) are more than four hours' distant from a large city."[5] Barja and Gigler argue that we need to assess this factor at a more local level, and to contextualize it in terms of other national factors (such as reach of the network, ability to use the technology, connectivity issues and relevant content) – which combined, allow for a national-level baseline measurement of information poverty, and a possible calculation of national level cost for its eradication. This level of detail is imperative for effective and realistic pro-poor strategy formulation for access gaps.

---

[5] Chomitz, Piet Buys and Thomas (2005).

2. Extending the Network's Reach

2.1. MOBILE TELEPHONY

As is well-documented, the growth of the mobile network worldwide during the past decade has achieved in expansion of access to the telecom network what years of universal service programs have failed to deliver. Mobile telephony has proven effective in developing economies because it is increasingly affordable and flexible. Further, the fact of pro-poor use of available telecom infrastructure has actually altered the economics of telecom provision, forcing the pervasiveness of a low average revenue per user for the market segment. Prepaid, shared use of handsets, texting, ring-call-back, and micro-financing of service vendors are some of the strategies that the poor use to make access to the telecom network affordable. It is these kinds of strategies that have made mobile telephony ubiquitous in countries that are still unable to provide adequate fixed-line infrastructure.

By the early 21st century, mobile expansion was no longer such a surprise, and the question of mobile telephony overtaking fixed line became a question of *when* rather than *if*. For Latin America, this happened in 2001. In early 2005, there were 176 million mobile phones in Latin America – compared with 92 million fixed line phones.[6] As noted by Mariscal et al. (chapter 3) mobile telephony is the predominant form of network access by the poor in the LA&C region.

The initial surge of mobile expansion occurred during a period of liberalization and opening up of markets. In order to attract investment in these markets, there was a high degree of concern to demonstrate regulatory oversight on issues such as interconnection, competition and level playing fields for service provision. Mobile service provision was typically the first segment of the telecom market to be open to competition in most countries; and there were national level advantages to providing sufficient conditions to attract investment.

Now, however, as documented by Mariscal et al., many Latin American national markets are undergoing strong consolidation of service provision – which has bearing on affordability of services, and in some instances on provision of new services. Further, concurrent to the rapid growth rate for mobile telephony, and to some extent because of it, there has been a stagnation of fixed line roll-out.

In Latin America, fixed line teledensity hovers around 17%. Further, an issue with relying on mobile telephony for network extension is that unless you are connected to the network via expensive satellite services the signal does not reach far off of the beaten track of fixed line services. Especially for rural connectivity solutions, other wireless technologies could be useful to extend access points to other users and to

---

[6] BuddeComm (2005).

remote communities. A weak point for mobile services concerns interconnection with other networks – and long distance and roaming charges. Thus, the benefits of gaining access to the network can be limited to a particular service range.

Further, there is also the paramount issue of access to information services and content, fundamental for participation in the information society and economy. As was the case with prepaid mobile telephony, new wireless technologies have the potential to further alter economic models of telecom service provision – making them more accessible to the poor and marginalized. But because of spectrum requirements, many of the new technology applications require particular regulatory conditions, if not active regulatory support. Clearly there will be points of contradiction between creating regulatory incentives for robust network roll-out of fixed line services; and new ownership and open access models which will compete with the offering of these services.

The ICT needs of the region are diverse – falling along a spectrum of initiatives to meet the Millennium Development Goals (MDGs) to attaining enhanced e-commerce capabilities. For the former, access to the telecom network infrastructure is a good first step, but for all points on the spectrum, there is a range of new technologies with potential to meet different levels of connectivity needs.

2.2. OTHER NETWORK SOLUTIONS

The most prominent of new wireless technology solutions is the WiFi protocol which can be used to create a wireless local area network for users to access the Internet. Because of its range being limited to about 150 meters (at permitted power levels of transmission) WiFi has mostly been deployed in urban areas to extend access to the Internet in both commercial and community non-profit settings. However, using point-to-point antennas, there are clear advantages for deploying WiFi in rural community settings.

Worldwide Interoperability for Microwave Access (WiMax) is an emerging protocol in the same vein as WiFi – but offering a range of 35-40 kilometers, much higher bandwidth.[7] Millicom Argentina and Colombia Telecom have both deployed *pre*WiMAX networks.[8] CorDECT building on the EU's DECT[9] standard, and other fixed wireless local loop solutions are being used to provide high quality voice and always on Internet. Like WiFi and WiMAX, the range of up to 35 kilometers can be extended with a repeater station. (See Mallalieu and Rocke chapter 6 for a detailed list of pro-poor ICT solutions.)

---

[7] For an overview of WiMAX spectrum requirements, see Fellah (2005) and Kahn (2003).

[8] The equipment used cannot be certified as WiMAX – because the standard is still being developed.

[9] Digital European Cordless Telephone (DECT).

There are varying restrictions on the use of the WiFi band of spectrum in terms of how and by whom the necessary spectrum can be used. Some countries offer free use up to 1 Watt, others impose relatively onerous and expensive registration requirements. For regulators (and indeed for telecom service providers) the advent of protocols such as WiFi and WiMAX blurs the distinction between traditional telephony and information services provision. With Internet access, individuals can access services and applications such as voice over IP (VoIP) because voice services are otherwise not available or because VoIP telephony is cheaper. Also, benefits of VoIP are becoming evident in terms of decreasing international revenue settlements.

Regulation of VoIP service provision is inconsistent across Latin America – with some regulators designating the service as value-added and others as a voice service. Established service providers, especially for long distance services view VoIP as cheap competition undermining revenues. Some countries in the region prohibit VoIP, others require licensing, and in others it is either deregulated or not regulated as a value-added service (see Galperin and Girard chapter 5 for details on LA&C licensing conditions).

These three IP convergence examples (WiFi, WiMAX and VoIP) provide evidence of the unbundling of network services from network infrastructure (see Figure 1), and significantly reduce barriers to entry in services provisioning. While mobile and

Figure 1: **ICT Service Layers**

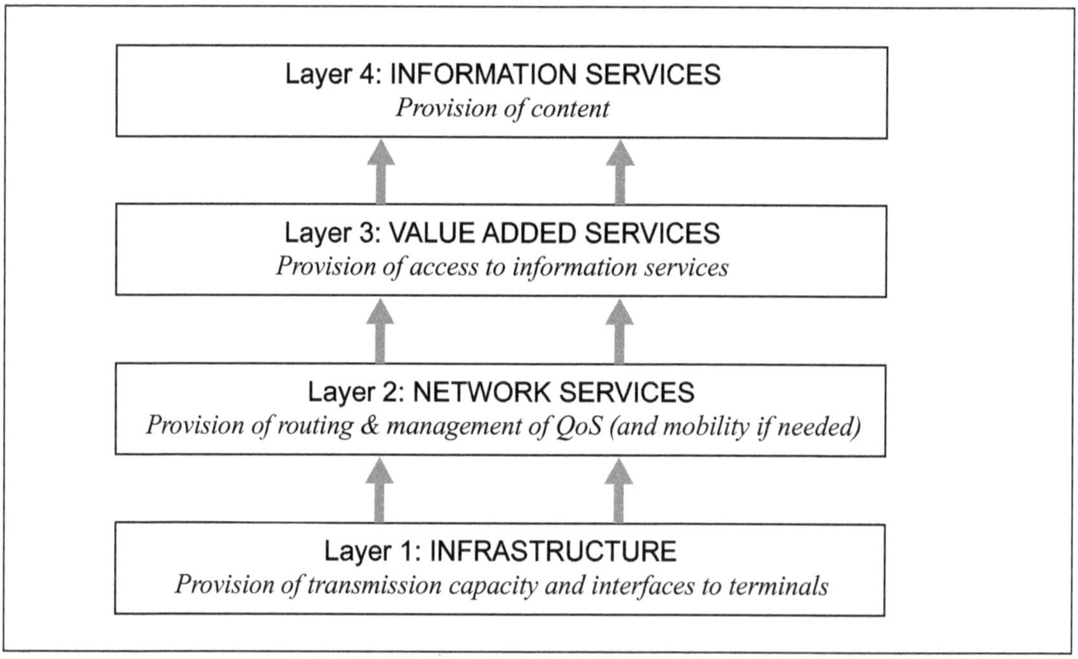

Source: Arnbak (1999).

prepaid mobile rocked the market for extending individuals' access to the network, internet protocol services drastically expand the possibilities for diversifying participation in network development. Given regulatory conditions that will allow new modes of connectivity to flourish, existing traditional operators will be challenged with assessing their business models and strategies for identifying new market segments. It is not difficult to imagine resistance to this task.

In a completely different vein of innovation, Powerline Transmission (PLT) is the use of electricity wiring (and electricity grid infrastructure) for communications and data transmission. Powerline technology has been long used by power companies for internal communication and for the monitoring of their infrastructure. PLT for more widespread use has been under research since the mid-1990s, with different versions currently on trial in some 30 countries.[10] The underlying components of digital powerline technology involve adapters to change the data into frequencies to be carried along the electricity current, and a modem which subsequently separates data from electricity. Thus, the network that is deployed is as ubiquitous as the location's energy provision. This has huge implications for using shared resources for extending ICT access for many remote regions where lack of telecom services is coupled with lack of power supply.

2.3. BALANCING REGULATORY STRATEGIES

Given the potential of emerging technologies to alter the economics of telecom provision, their deployment is bound to be contested by established telco providers, which is a particularly pernicious factor if there is opportunity for regulatory capture. On the other hand, the roll-out of fixed line services is still of paramount importance, especially for broadband, and regulators must balance requirements for attracting investment in this regard – which includes guarantees of return on investment, and hence a certain market exclusivity. Thus while there are immediate solutions which can be undertaken, and indeed which are essential for meeting immediate connectivity needs, these should not preclude development of long-term more robust solutions using conventional fixed wire connectivity. Table 2 lists some trade-offs involved in different regulatory paths.

An important question here is whether IP and new wireless solutions will become sufficiently robust to supplant traditional fixed line ICT infrastructure. This has not been the case for mobile (and especially prepaid) telephony, which offers a lesser quality service and is limited in terms of future information applications. But, if the answer to the future of WiMAX in particular is promising, then this opens up

---

[10] Plugtek.com maintains a website with links to current articles and company press releases about PLT developments. <http://www.plugtek.com/index.shtml>

Table 2: **Benefits of Licensed and License-exempt Solutions**

Licensed Solution Advantages	License-Exempt Solution Advantages
Better quality of service	Faster rollout
Better non-line-of-sight reception at lower frequencies	Lower costs
Higher barriers for entrance	More worldwide options

Source: Intel (2005).

a new set of options for communities, beyond temporary arrangements while waiting for the real network to come. Different models of community service provision (or *microtelcos*) are discussed in the chapter by Galperin and Girard (chapter 5). They address the new range of questions and issues that are raised for regulators who are charged with respecting license conditions while simultaneously promoting universal access. As regulators allow and work with communities to adopt affordable solutions, the resulting bypass of traditional network infrastructure may create precedents, termed *unfair competition* by traditional service providers.

Regulatory logic of level playing fields for competition has resulted in a framework which continues to allow private sector actors to not serve unprofitable communities. However, overall economic health requires increased connectivity for all segments of the population. In the same vein, there is a dimension of entitlement in communication rights and access to ICT. Given information economy imperatives (e-readiness) and the advent of new technologies with their potential to alter the locus of provisioning and control of ICT services and access, the notion of flexible regulation takes on increased importance. Further, the lesson of mobile telephony deployment bridging the nexus of access and market efficiency gaps, is that with emerging technologies, inevitable changes to the service provision market are on the horizon.

3. Universal Access Programs and Diversifying Participation in Network Development

Based on the discussion of new technologies and their disruptive potential – both for providing new means of connectivity and in terms of the economics of traditional telecom service provision, we begin to see how different regulatory options can skew or flatten the playing field. For the foreseeable future, however, it is argued that the current arrangement of government policies and spending, and private sector investment will continue to be the main national level drivers of ICT infrastructure roll-out and modernization. Innovation and adoption of new technologies will also be led by government best practice and a healthy market. Many Latin American government-owned telecom monopolies prior to privatization were under-funded and badly managed, and the initial impetus of privatization and simultaneous introduction of competition in the mobile sector have done much to drive down prices, shorten or eliminate waiting lists and extend infrastructure.[11] There are still, however, communities and members of the population who have not yet benefited from privatization.

By 2006, it is estimated that only 6% of the Latin American population will have access to the Internet. Physical access, especially for difficult to reach network locations, is only one aspect of extending services. Marginalized communities that are not connected to the network and which are already isolated, will also need programs which support training for applications and general awareness raising about the new connectivity generally. In a similar vein, there must be attention to content development and availability of information and services, such as those provided by government. Increasingly there is a realization that access programs need to be built up from the community. Access through leased lines and shared community resources will be the main vehicles of growth for the region. It is at this level that access to what kinds of services can be best determined and subsequently mobilized.

Given emerging technologies, and the particularities of Latin American markets, how should universal access programs be designed and assessed? For the latter, as noted above, there are increasingly dynamic indicators which can be applied to assess both the level and effectiveness of connectivity. Likewise, design of such programs is also becoming more nuanced, taking into account the imperative of *first mile* solutions and community consultation.

However, as noted earlier, the starting point for the design of universal access

---

[11] There are notable exceptions such as Uruguay which continues to provide world class telecom services, having to date resisted privatization trends.

programs is accurate assessment of the regulatory and market terrain. Access gaps must be clearly identified as such. Given the project of regulation and competition, the first line of attack must weed out market inefficiency and hence focus on incentives for operators, license conditions and devices such as build-operate-transfer arrangements. In other words, the strategies must first focus on creating conditions for private sector initiatives and investment through market mechanisms.

The second line of attack then is charged with remedying true access gaps for potential users. Programs in this vein will include cooperatives and community owned projects, micro credit financing programs and rural development funds. Countries in Latin America that currently support such programs include:

- Chile, Fondo de Desarrollo de las Telecomunicaciones (government budget);

- Peru, Fondo de Inversión en Telecomunicaciones (FITEL) (1% operator levy);

- Colombia, Fondo de Comunicaciones (Compartel) (5% operator levy and government contribution);

- Guatemala, Fondo para el Desarrollo de la Telefonía (FONDETEL) (spectrum auctions);

- Dominican Republic, Fondo de Desarrollo de las Telecomunicaciones (FDT) (2% operator levy); and

- Argentina, Brazil, Bolivia, Ecuador and Nicaragua, which are also in various stages of implementing USO funds.[12]

The programs are as varied as their funding arrangements, reflecting different regulatory and market environments. Access programs are essential for addressing some of the network externality issues such as content creation, training and software development. However, as discussed by Galperin and Girard, many instances of access failure could be addressed by proactive regulation, permitting an organic uptake of connectivity – driven by need and desire for access to information and services, and achieved using emerging technology solutions.

Much of the above has focused on pro-poor strategies for connecting potential users to the network. But there must also be attention to consumers, especially to ensure that low profit sectors of the market are adequately served. Poor quality of service, unfair pricing, failure to maintain or continue to invest in infrastructure, and so forth are all possible in developing infrastructure situations. This is

---

[12] Intelecon (2005).

especially likely if consumers are unaware of their rights or are unclear about how to exercise them, or if the regulatory environment is weak and ineffective.

By way of example, affordability was not initially the case for mobile telephony. When pre-paid services were first offered they were intended as a niche market for the then affluent mobile phone users – and were priced accordingly. Although posing much lower levels of risk for default on payments and freeing-up the service provider from billing and collection administration, originally pre-paid was much more expensive than subscription arrangements. A less affluent, but massive market soon became apparent and the costs of prepaid mobile telephony came down, resulting in the pervasive expansion of telecom infrastructure.[13] But, this would not have happened outside of a competitive environment – designed to lower prices and provide incentives to affordably extend the network.

Further, where mobile telephony is the predominant network access point, then questions of quality of service become paramount, as users risk being trapped in a lower quality stand-in for fixed line access.

In a different example, it has been argued that high standards of quality of service (for example imposed at the introduction of privatization and competition) are inhibiting factors for extending service to the poor. In particular, some of the inherited standards (in many instances, a photocopy of regulation devised for developed countries) may not necessarily correspond to developing country contexts which may require low cost, small scale, alternative, community level provision. Thus, the notion of "quality diversification"[14] – a relaxation of some rigorous quality standards in order to be able to provide cheaper services to the poor – is presumed as a better option than no service at all. Without some oversight and recourse, it is easy to imagine classes of users being trapped in substandard service provision, even when upgrades become technologically and economically feasible.

Efforts to extend ICT networks to the poor and marginalized must be accompanied by subsequent protection and support of their rights in this regard. Dussán and Roldán (chapter 4) discuss the origins of a telecom Ombudsman. They also propose a survey to be administered to regulators, consumers and telecom providers to inform future regulation – especially for disenfranchised sectors of the population who are also consumers of network services. With such information, efforts to ensure that pro-poor regulation is also forward-looking become more sound.

---

[13] However, subscription based mobile services on average are still cheaper than prepaid services for local and long distance calling.

[14] For a description and justification of this idea, see Baker and Trémolet (2000).

4. REDIS-DIRSI – Moving into the Future

All good research concludes with directions for further investigation. Accordingly, this collection of REDIS-DIRSI research provides stellar pointers for continuing current research and new paths for future exploration. The book is organized around three general areas: indicators and assessment; consumer protection and the context of market concentration mitigating the effects of regulatory reform and privatization; and the role of new technologies and community ownership in extending service provision opportunities.

Two chapters in this volume propose new methodologies for obtaining a clearer perspective on the current status of Information Society in LA&C – with a particular focus on who is excluded from this picture. Barrantes' *digital poverty* methodology has been applied in Peru to better inform policy formulation and decision-making; and both this and the *information poverty* assessment methodology designed by Barja can be tested in different countries across the region.

Dussán and Roldán propose a survey to assess the regulatory terrain – giving voice to all stakeholders. The particular interest here is to work towards more effective intervention and protection of consumer rights. This work is informed by Mariscal's assessment of the role of the market in Latin America, and contending with the continent's current duopoly situation.

Galperin and Girard detail new ownership models and possibilities for community provision of network services. This work provides evidence of highly replicable models. The Percolator Model outline in Mallalieu and Rocke (chapter 6) will further inform community choices of appropriate technology.

The publication of this work is the first concerted effort of the REDIS-DIRSI research network. Due to financial support from the Institute of Connectivity of the Americas (ICA-IDRC – International Development Research Centre) the network anticipates moving ahead along these themes, within the rubric of the network's designated scope of activities and established research agenda (see Foreword).

References

Arnbak, J. (1999). Policy Priorities for Information Infrastructure Development. *Research Workshop on "Telematics and the Economy of Information Societies"* February 5-6, Zoetermeer, The Netherlands.

Baker, B. & Trémolet, S. (2000). Regulating quality standards to improve access for the poor. *Public Policy for the Private Sector*, Note No. 219. Washington DC: World Bank.

BuddeComm. (2005). *Latin America-Telecomm. Market, Regulatory and Infrastructure Overview*. Paul Budde Communication Pty Ltd.

Chomitz, K., Buys, P. & Thomas, T. (2005). Quantifying the Rural-Urban Gradient in Latin America and the Caribbean. *Policy Research Working Paper* 3634 Washington DC: World Bank. Retrieved from http://www-wds.worldbank.org/servlet/WDS_IBank_Servlet?pcont= details&eid=000016406_20050614122820

Daly, J. (2004). *The Institutional Divide: Is The Digital Divide a Symptom or a Cause?* Retrieved from http://topics.developmentgateway.org/ict/rc/filedownload.do~itemId=102604

Economist Intelligence Unit. (2005). *The 2005 e-readiness Rankings.* The Economist Intelligence Unit and The IBM Institute for Business Value. Retrieved from http://graphics.eiu.com/files/ad_pdfs/2005Ereadiness_Ranking_WP.pdf

ENAHO (Encuesta Nacional de Hogares). (2004). Lima, Peru: Instituto Nacional de Estadística e Informática.

Estache, A. (2004). Emerging Infrastructure Policy Issues in Developing Countries: A Survey of the Recent Economic Literature. *Policy Research Working Paper 3442.* Washington DC: The World Bank. Retrieved from http://ideas.repec.org/p/wbk/wbrwps/3442.html

Estache, A., Manacorda, M. & Tommaso, V. (2002). Telecommunication Reforms, Access Regulation, and Internet Adoption in Latin America. *Policy Research Working Paper 2802.* Washington DC: The World Bank.

Fellah, A. (2005). The WiMAX Spectrum Picture, *WiMAX Trends.* Retrieved from http://www.wimax-trends.com/articles/feature/f032805a.htm

Guislain, P. (2004). *Telecommunication: Legal, Policy and Regulatory Framework and World Bank Experience.* Washington DC: The World Bank.

Henten, A., Samarajiva, R. & Melody, W.H. (2003). *Report on the WDR Dialogue Theme 2002, Designing Next Generation Telecom Regulation: ICT Convergence or Multisector Utility?* Lyngby: The World Dialogue on Regulation for Network Economies (WDR). Retrieved from http://www.regulateonline.org/content/view/215/31/

Intel. (2005). *Deploying License-Exempt WiMAX Solutions.* White Paper, The Intel Corporation. Retrieved from http://www.intel.com/netcomms/technologies/wimax/306013.pdf

Intelecon. (2004). *Universal Access Funds.* Intelecon Research & Consultancy Ltd. Retrieved from http://www.inteleconresearch.com/pages/reports.html

Intelecon. (2005). *Universal Access and Universal Service Funds: Insights and experience of international best practice.* Intelecon Research & Consultancy. Retrieved July, from http://www.inteleconresearch.com/pages/reports.html

Kahn, K.C. (2003). On spectrums and standards, architecture and access points. *The Wireless Internet Opportunity for Developing Countries. The Wireless Internet Institute* (editors, *info*Dev, UNICT and Wireless Internet Institute). Retrieved from http://www.infodev.org/symp2003/publications/wired.pdf

Minges, M. (2005). *Measuring Digital Opportunity.* Seoul: International Telecommunication Union (ITU). Retrieved June, from http://www.itu.int/osg/spu/statistics/DOI/linkeddocs/Measuring_Digital_Opp_Final_Aug_29.pdf

Navas-Sabater, J. (2005). *Universal Access & Output-based Aid in Telecomm and ICT.* Global ICT Department. Washington DC: The World Bank. Retrieved from http://www-wds.worldbank.org/servlet/WDS_IBank_Servlet?pcont=details&eid= 000094946_02041804225061

Navas-Sabater, J., Dymond, A. & Juntunen, N. (2002). *Telecommunications and Information Services for the Poor: Toward a Strategy for Universal Access.* Washington DC: The World Bank. Retrieved from http://www.un.int/unitar/patit/NYtraining/seminar3/TELECOMANDINFO.PDF

NTIA. (1999). Falling Through the Net: *Defining the Digital Divide, A Report on the Telecommunications and Information Technology Gap in America.* National Telecommunications and Information Administration (NTIA). Retrieved from http://www.ntia.doc.gov/ntiahome/fttn99/FTTN.pdf

TeleCommons Development Group. (2002). *Towards Universal Telecom Access for Rural and Remote Communities.* TeleCommons Development Group. Retrieved from http://www.telecommons.com/reports.cfm?itemid=260

About the authors

Gover Barja, PhD, is director of the master's program in public policy at the Bolivian Catholic University in La Paz. He has researched and written on Bolivia's experience with reform on infrastructure industries for the World Institute for Development Economics Research (WIDER), the Economic Commission for Latin America and the Caribbean (ECLAC) and the Center for Global Development (CGD), and on macroeconomic performance for the Inter-American Development Bank (IADB) and poverty impacts for the Global Development Network (GDN). He is also consultant for the Bolivian Government, the Bolivian Regulatory System, the World Bank and the Andean Community. An important area of his research and consulting has been on the Bolivian telecommunications industry, its regulation, universal access for rural areas and ICT for development and competitiveness. He received his PhD in economics and MS in statistics from Utah State University.

Björn-Sören Gigler is a PhD candidate at the Development Studies Institute at the London School of Economics and Political Science (LSE), United Kingdom. Currently he is working as an ICT for Development Specialist at the Informatics Department at the World Bank. In the academic year 2004/2005 he was an Assistant Professor for Development Studies at the Universidad Católica Boliviana in La Paz, Bolivia. In 2003/2004 he was a Graduate Teaching Assistant at the Government and Information Systems Departments at the LSE. From 1997–2003 he worked as an information officer and consultant at the Social Development Unit at the World Bank. He holds an MSc (International Economics) from the Ludwig-Maximilian University of Munich, Germany and an MA (International Relations) from the George Washington University, USA. Sören's main research interest is the perspective of indigenous peoples on human well-being and development. He is particularly interested in operationalizing Amartya Sen's capability approach and to apply it to indigenous peoples in the Latin American context.

Roxana Barrantes, PhD, is currently a research associate at the Instituto de Estudios Peruanos, and a member of its board of directors. Dr Barrantes has previously worked for the Telecommunications Regulator in Peru both as a staff and board member. She has also worked as a consultant for the Peruvian Ministry of Communications on different policy issues. She obtained her PhD in Economics at the University of Illinois at Urbana-Champaign. Her recent publications include: La regulación para el desarrollo de las telecomunicaciones en el Perú: 1993–2001, 2005, Japan Center for Area Studies Occasional Paper N° 25. JCAS-IEP series viii. Osaka; Balance de la investigación económica y social en el Perú 1999–2003, 2004, Consorcio de Investigación Económica y Social, Serie Diagnóstico y Propuesta # 15, Lima. Escrito con Javier Iguíñiz; Tributación online. En busca de una mayor equidad contributiva (online). Lima: Instituto de Estudios Peruanos, 2003, rev. 5 de julio de 2004. Disponible en: http://www.icamericas.net/modules/DownloadsPlus/uploads/Estudios_de_caso_y_Reportes/TributacionOnline-Integrado-Spanish.pdf. Escrito con Juan José Miranda.

Julio César Luna finished his undergraduate studies in Economics at the Instituto Tecnológico Autónomo de México (ITAM). From 2003 to 2006 he worked as a research assistant in the CIDE's Telecommunications program, participating in various projects. Now Julio César is carrying out field research on ICT issues in the State of Chiapas.

Judith Mariscal, PhD, has extensive research experience in Information and Communications Technologies focusing on public policy and regulatory issues. She is currently a professor of the Public Administration Department at the "Centro de Investigación y Docencia Económicas (CIDE)", an independent research and educational institution based in Mexico City. As director of CIDE's Telecommunications program Dr Mariscal monitors various research assignments with special emphasis on projects dealing with pro-poor ICT policies and the information society. She also teaches graduate courses as part of CIDE's Public Administration Department faculty. Dr Mariscal holds a doctorate degree on Public Policy from the LBJ School of Public Affairs of the University of Texas at Austin, a Master's degree on International Economic Policy from CIDE, and a BSc in Economics from the ITAM. She has authored numerous articles on telecommunications policy and regulation, as well as the book "Unfinished Business: Telecommunications Reform in Mexico" (Praeger Press, 2002).

Carla Marisa Bonina is the Academic Development Coordinator of the Telecommunications Research Program, Telecom-CIDE, at the Centro de Investigación y Docencia Económicas (CIDE) in Mexico City. She holds a B.S. in Economics at the University of Buenos Aires and an MPPA from CIDE and the LBJ School at the University of Texas at Austin. Her current studies focus on

ICT for development, telecommunications regulation and e-government. She has collaborated on numerous articles with Judith Mariscal and other researchers from CIDE. Her last publication was *"Mobile Communications in Mexico: A first look at usage patterns"* coauthored with Judith Mariscal and to be published soon as a book chapter in *Mainstreaming Mobiles*, James Katz (Ed.), MIT Press, (Forthcoming).

Hernan Galperin, PhD, is Assistant Professor at the Annenberg School for Communication at the University of Southern California (USA) and Research Associate at the Universidad de San Andrés (Argentina). Dr Galperin is also affiliated with the Stanhope Centre for Communications Policy Research (UK) and the Edelstein Center for Social Research (Brazil). His research and teaching focus on the international governance and impact of new information and communication technologies. Currently, Dr Galperin is involved in a number of research projects related to the development impact and poverty alleviation potential of new information and communication technologies in Latin America, funded by a variety of foundations and international organizations. He has published extensively in major journals such as *Telecommunications Policy*, *The Information Society*, the *Journal of Communication*, and *Information Technologies and International Development*. Dr Galperin is a member of the Steering Committee of the Regional Dialogue on the Information Society (REDIS-DIRSI). He obtained his PhD at Stanford University.

Bruce Girard is a researcher, educator and activist. His work covers a broad number of communications areas, including communication for development, participatory communication, broadcasting, communication rights and ICT applications and policy. He coordinates the Comunica network and directs communication strategy for the World Dialogue on Regulation. His books include The One to Watch: Radio, New ICTs and Interactivity, Global Media Governance (with Seán Ó Siochrú and Amy Mahan), and Communicating in the Information Society.

Jorge Dussán Hitscherich is a Lawyer at the Pontificia Universidad Javeriana, specializing in Trade Law in the same University, with experience of fifteen years in Administrative law, advanced studies of directive development (PDD) at the "Alta Dirección Empresarial" Institute – INALDE. He was attending at the Constituent National Assembly and has been advisor for the Ministry of Communications (1993–1995), for the Superintendencia de Servicios Públicos Domiciliarios authority (1995–1997) and for the Comisión de Regulación de Telecomunicaciones (1997–1998). From January 1999 to September 2002 he was "Expert of the Comisión de Regulación de Telecomunicaciones". He has been head teacher of Public Services at the Pontificia Universidad Javeriana and teacher of Telecommunications Law at the Universities of Rosario and Jorge Tadeo Lozano. At the moment he works as a consultant for private telecommunications companies and is member of DIRSI. He is author of *"Elementos del contrato estatal"* and *"Régimen de los servicios públicos domiciliarios"*, as well as several articles on Administrative Law and Telecommunications (www.dussan.net/www.dussan.blogspot.com).

Juan Manuel Roldán Perea is an Electrical Engineer with a Master's in Economics from Universidad de los Andes, Colombia. He currently works as advisor for the Comisión de Regulación de Telecomunicaciones (CRT – www.crt.gov.co). He is an Associate Professor at the Physics and Electrical Engineering Department at the same university.

Kim Mallalieu, PhD, is the initiator and coordinator of the online Master's degree program in Telecommunications Regulation and Policy, MRP (Telecommunications), at the St Augustine campus of The University of the West Indies, UWI. She is a Fulbright Fellow and an alumnus of the Massachusetts Institute of Technology and the University of London. Dr Mallalieu is a tenured senior lecturer in The UWI's Department of Electrical and Computer Engineering where she leads its academic and commercial programs in Communication Systems. She has a keen interest in the development of Web-based gaming for education and in community informatics. In the latter capacity, she is a member of DIRSI, Diálogo Regional sobre Sociedad de la Información. Kim is the recipient of local and international teaching and service awards. She has written numerous academic publications and has sat on a variety of advisory, technical and academic committees, at home and abroad. These include the Board of the Telecommunications Authority of Trinidad and Tobago and the Editorial Advisory Board of the *International Journal of Electrical Engineering Education*.

Sean A. Rocke has been involved in Data Communications and Computer Systems for the last decade. Within that period he attained his BSc in Electrical and Computer Engineering from the University of the West Indies in Trinidad and Tobago. He has since worked on industrial data communications networks and provided various support services to the University of the West Indies under the guidance of Dr Kim Mallalieu. He consequently went on to pursue his Masters in Communications Management at Coventry University. Upon his return he resumed work with Dr Mallalieu aimed at promulgating their mutual interests in ICT-related development. He is currently an Assistant Lecturer at the University of the West Indies under the Communications Systems Group in the Department of Electrical and Computer Engineering. His research areas of interest are in Digital Signal Processing with focus upon Mobile Systems, Speech and Image Processing, Optical Networks, Virtual Organisation, Sustainable application of eCommerce Technologies particularly to health and education, as well as other ICT-related Developmental Issues.

Amy Mahan is a senior researcher and in charge of publications for LIRNE.NET <www.lirne.net> and the World Dialogue on Regulation for Network Economies <www.regulate online.org>. Working and living in Montevideo, Uruguay, she is engaged in an initiative to extend the activities of these two research networks into the Latin America and Caribbean region. Current research themes include ICT for development and regulatory institutional practices, with recent work focusing on information provision practices and communication with ICT stakeholders, including consumer and pro-poor policy advocates, and concerned with the processes and conditions affecting how informed and effective participation is encouraged by the regulatory authority. Recent books include: *Stimulating Investment in Network Development: Roles for Regulators* (World Dialogue on Regulation for Network Economies, 2005, co-editor with W.H. Melody); *Virtual Consulate Primer: How to design and implement an e-Visa programme* (UNDP, 2005, contributing author and editor); *How to Build Open Information Societies* (UNDP, 2004, co-editor with Yuri Misnikov); *Networking Knowledge for Information Societies: Institutions & Intervention* (Delft University Press, 2002, co-editor with Robin Mansell and Rohan Samarajiva); and *Global Media Governance: A beginner's Guide* (Rowman & Littlefield, 2002, co-author with Sean O Siochru and Bruce Girard).

Network Facilitator:

Francisco Gutierrez is Network Facilitator of the Regional Dialogue on the Information Society (REDIS-DIRSI). Currently, Francisco is involved in a number of projects related to ICTs and development as The Latin American Network of Digital Cities (www.iberomunicipios.net), evaluating e-readiness of national and local governments in the region. He also collaborates with PROTIC.org an initiative developed by The Institute for Connectivity in the Americas (ICA), The Economic Commission for Latin America (CEPAL) and Red Colombiana de Comunicación (COLNODO).